B2B Sales Appointment Strategies

JUSTIN CHUGG

Copyright © 2020 Justin Chugg

All rights reserved.

DEDICATION

None of this would be possible without the constant strength and encouragement of my dear wife Florcita, my kids: Florcita, Wilfred, Elias, Charity, and Ephraim

CONTENTS

	Introduction	Pg 7
1	Referral Partners	Pg 8
2	Lead Exchanges	Pg 21
3	List Building	Pg 28
4	LinkedIn	Pg 35
5	Appointments Setting	Pg 51
6	Sales Intelligence	Pg 109
7	Meeting Strategies	Pg 116
8	Practical Approach	Pg 124
9	Conclusion	Pg 131

INTRODUCTION

The purpose of this book is to help share the latest and greatest sales strategies in order to keep up with the ever-evolving challenges facing B2B sales reps.

The ultimate goal of this work is to find the fastest and most efficient path to sales appointments.

CHAPTER 1: REFERRAL PARTNERS

The greatest sales strategy will always involve referral partners. Referral partners create customer acquisition multipliers replicating your efforts which is only **compounded** with a good sales strategy (we'll get to that later).

Typically, when people describe referral relationships, they use the image of a two-way street. One partner sends a deal and the other partner refers a deal back. While this model does work, **there is a better way** to run referral relationships. If you want a superior referral relationship, you're going to need to build a **converging one-way street**.

A **one-way referral relationship** is structured **differently** than traditional two-way referral relationships. Rather than throwing deals back and forth, a one-way referral relationship is more **strategic**. The two referral partners compliment, depend, and **strengthen one another**. An example would include someone who sells phones and another company who supplies bandwidth. The two products complement each other. The best types of referral relationships enables the partners to sell different products to the same client in the same transaction.

The following examples will further illustrate the nature of one-way referral relationships:

Government Referral Partners: Each state, county, and city typically have goals and incentives to attract new businesses and jobs to their local area. Typically, there are direct, indirect, formal, and informal incentives for businesses who to move to the area. It's worthwhile to reach out to your local office of economic development (city, county, state, and national) to ask about their goals. **Find out what type of incentives they have** in place and how to recommend/introduce potential companies.

Once you understand your economic development office's goals and prospects, it's time to begin reaching out to companies that meet these criteria. It is not always required for these organizations to move their offices; rather simply build a new location. It may be worthwhile to engage a business consultant as a referral partner to help execute these conversations. Not only will this relationship help you scale your efforts, but form a profitable partnership on future opportunities. As you engage company prospects, you can build a relationship with your economic development group by sharing your progress.

Here are a few examples of incentives government agencies offer businesses:

- Through **annual** investments of up to $100 million, the Clean Transportation Program, formerly known as the Alternative and Renewable Fuels and Vehicle Technology Program, promotes accelerated development and deployment of advanced transportation and fuel technologies. The program was established by Assembly Bill 118 (Núñez, 2007), which took effect January 1 2008, and was extended through January 1, 2024 by Assembly Bill 8 (Perea, 2013)

- Public Finance Authority (PFA)'s Industrial Development Bond Program provides eligible manufacturers with capital project financing for land, buildings, and new equipment through the issuance of tax-exempt industrial development bonds ("IDBs"). IDBs allow manufacturers to finance projects at a lower interest rate than conventional financing because the interest paid to the bondholders is exempt from federal income tax.

- Employment Training Panel (ETP): Provides funding to employers to assist in upgrading the skills of their workers through training that leads to good paying, long-term jobs. The ETP was created in 1982 by the California State Legislature and is funded by California employers through a special payroll tax. The ETP is a funding agency, not a training agency. Businesses determine their own training needs and how to provide training. ETP staff is available to assist in applying for funds and other aspects of participation.

- The Advanced Industries (AI) Export Accelerator Grant program is now accepting applications from current and aspiring Colorado exporters in the advanced industries who are looking to offset international business development and marketing costs. Grants are available for up to $15,000 for eligible costs for small and medium-sized AI businesses in aerospace, infrastructure engineering, advanced manufacturing, energy and natural resources, bioscience, electronics, and technology and information. Grants can be used to help cover the costs of trade missions and trade shows, translation services for a contract or official document, intellectual property protection, conducting due diligence or credit reviews on potential buyers or distributors, and production and design of international marketing materials.

- Industrial Revenue Bonds (IRBs) provide a source of tax-exempt or taxable bond finance for projects involving significant private activity that promote new and existing businesses, encourage employment, and expand the tax base of a community. IRBs are issued by Industrial

Development Corporations sponsored by a government unit, but their proceeds are passed on to private businesses, which are generally responsible for debt service payment.

In addition to partnering with business consultants, these grants and incentives provide ample room to have conversation with business investors to see if any of the companies within their portfolio would qualify.

Commercial Loan Officers: There is a natural synergy with banks for selling IT Security. Banks understand that the longevity of their clients will be in jeopardy **if the client does not safeguard their information technology**; which is why banks are the <u>number one source for IT security</u> leads. Partnering with loan officers makes their job easier by having a consistent relationship they can rely on to refer their clients. If your relationship becomes strategic enough, loan officers may even require your IT security services before securing a loan.

Commercial loan officers are also a crucial partner in financing the purchase of your products and projects. It is much easier to work with someone who understands the nuances of your business and avoid unnecessary finance roadblocks due to inexperience.

Insurance Brokers: Many businesses carry an insurance called **"Business Interruption Insurance"**. When disasters or accidents interrupt a business's workflow, they can rely on the **interruption insurance** to fill the gap. Insurance companies who offer this service do not offer disaster recovery solutions, but **highly recommend** and sometimes **require** their clients to use business continuity technologies to avoid using the business interruption insurance. In some instances, their monthly premium will be lowered when they can prove they have a viable business continuity solution in place.

Business continuity is one of the better products to focus on due to the vast scope of products required to create a complete business continuity solution. If your business focuses on only a few of the products needed to complete a disaster recovery solution, it would be an excellent opportunity to form a lead exchange of referral partners to help you accomplish your customer's goals and business continuity aspirations.

Customer Relationship Management Providers: One of the best examples of one-way referral relationships comes from CRM partnerships. In order to access cloud-based CRM data, you need good **bandwidth**. To optimize your bandwidth, you need an **SD-WAN provider**. Access to the CRM and the local network need to be **secured**. The company's business can help optimize workforce activities through CRM **integrations**. Software vendors can enhance the CRM's ability to communicate with third party applications.

In these examples it's easy to see how one referral partner **strengthens the other**. It's not about referring business back and forth, it's about being involved in every opportunity **together**, so that the chances of winning **increase** and your clients become **stickier**.

Below are a few examples of the most popular referral relationships:

- Commercial Loan Officers
- Managed Service Providers
- Direct Sales Reps
- Furniture Companies
- Collection Agencies
- Venture Capitalists
- Cabling Companies
- Business Consultants
- Architects
- CRM Providers
- Construction Companies
- Commercial Real-Estate Agents
- Interior Design
- Moving Companies
- Painters
- Carpet Companies
- Property Management
- Software Vendors

The opportunity to create a referral relationship should not be limited by a company's business model, but by **geography**. Your most successful referral relationships will come from **local companies**. Not only will working with local referral partners increase the commonalities that exist between you and the referral partner, but it will also **lower your overall customer acquisition costs**.

Working with local companies does limit the variety of partners you can work with, but with an **unconventional mindset**, finding the right referral partner shouldn't be difficult. There are two main categories of unconventional referral partners: **business to business** partners and **business to consumer** partners. It's easy to partner with each of these categories, but the strategies must be **different for each one**.

If your referral partner works in the **B2C** space, you will employ a **Group Purchasing strategy**. Without getting into too much detail (*see Chapter 5 for more details*), the B2C referral partners will form a **group purchasing community** where they can receive discounts on purchases and form their own referral network.

In the B2B realm it is much easier to form traditional referral relationships because everyone is in the business of acquiring business clients. Take some time to see how your strengths can help them. Even when you offer the same products, you may consider dividing up the city, or focusing on different size organizations, enabling each of you to specialize (hedgehog concept) in a different space and collaborate on business opportunities.

Once you identify the referral partners you want to work with, there are a few strategies that will help maximize the success of the partnership. Most referral relationships carry some type of financial incentive for each party. In a one-way referral relationship, **the value of the financial incentive is overshadowed by the value of the partner and their products**. This does not eliminate the need to provide financial incentives, but does provide the opportunity for a unique approach that will prove very powerful in the long run.

Rather than offering money, the most effective incentive is a "**Plan B**'. In many instances, it is not permitted to offer someone from another company financial incentives for business referrals. A Plan B solution not only overcomes this challenge, but offers a **far superior incentive**. Referral partners typically hold the position of a sales rep, which by nature is an **unstable job** (one of the highest turnover rates in any industry). A Plan B incentive is an independent bank account where money is deposited related to joint customer relationships. **If your referral partner loses their job, the bank account will made available to the referral partner**.

Not only does this provide the referral partner with a peace of mind, but it also provides the incentive of

financial freedom. The money can be offered on condition that they work for you, but as in independent contractor. Most sales reps love the idea of being in control of their destiny, but never have the financial means to become their own boss. This incentive helps restore not only the peace of mind they need to do their job knowing there is a **backup**, but provides a **long-term** incentive for them to gain **independence**.

Working with a referral partner also requires **buy in from the top**. There are two strategies that will enable you to engage and win over the **business owners** of your referral partners. The opening conversation should address what many business owners hope for: **the sale of their company**. The subject matter will not only **secure appointments more easily**, but demonstrate **the value of your partnership**. Most services today have been converted into a **monthly recurring cost**. When compared to one-off sales, monthly recurring sales are valued ten times **greater than traditional sales**. This in turn creates both **consistent** revenue and much higher **value** for your referral partner's business.

In addition to raising the value of their business, the most strategic relationship will involve becoming part of their organization. This doesn't mean you quit your day job, but it does imply making some changes. The second approach is easy to pursue. When your potential referral partner is looking to expand their sales team, **apply for the job**. Once you begin the application process, explain that you are willing to **work for free** because their product and your product complement each other so well that there is no need to pay you. As you sell your core product, you will also sell their product.

Essentially you join their sales team **by going to market together**. You **pursue the same clients**, but work together on closing the deal by **combining your product sets**. This in turn gives you a more intimate relationship with the business and their clients. This is much **more strategic**, but if you are unable to get permission from your employer to take this route there are a few alternatives.

Referral relationships take time to build trust, but there are a few **shortcuts**. The goal behind the partnership is to **share the burden of acquiring customers**. Often times your referral partners will have a long history of clients. It's not easy to get access to existing clients right away, but the alternatives may be just as good.

In the advance people search on LinkedIn is an option to see the connections of an individual (see below).

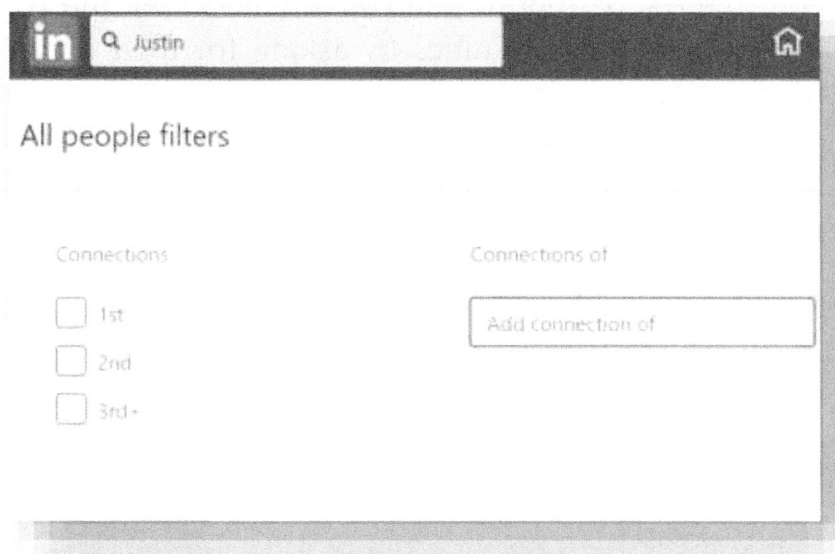

By looking up the connections of your referral partner, you will begin to see their **LinkedIn relationships and customers**. There is a certain degree of momentum and energy built into each of their client relationships. Contacting these relationships may cause some alarm, but contacting the **competitors and neighbors** of these connections will be beneficial to both of you. With the help of a few savvy internet tools, we can identify the competitors/neighbors of these clients. Free **competitor/neighbor** lists can be found on Zoom Info or ensable.com/data. You may also find a list of clients in the testimonial section of their website and on their Google maps page under **reviews**.

As you prospect into these opportunities, you can ask

your referral partner to join you and help you find your way into the opportunities by asking for their existing relationships to vouch for the (or at least permission to mention the competitor's/neighbor's name). It would also be wise to have them share with you a list of **past clients**.

CHAPTER 2: FORMING A LEAD EXCHANGE

The only thing better than referral relationships is a **lead exchange**. Typically, a lead exchange requires a level of trust that can only come with **time**, but can also evolve and **grow within the lead exchange**.

So, what is a lead exchange and how is it different from traditional referral partners? **The primary difference between these two models is accountability**. In a traditional referral relationship, influence, social pressure, and incentives drive the relationships. Lead exchange groups are driven by group **quotas**.

The most common characteristic of a lead exchange involves a **joint sales campaign**. The members that make up a lead exchange tend to be specialists in their field, enabling them to **compliment** team members **rather than compete** with them. It's also both common and necessary that lead exchange members take a **proactive** sales role (this is where the accountability comes in).

There are three types of lead exchanges:

1. Geographic Lead Exchanges
2. Vertical Lead Exchanges

3. Product Lead Exchanges

A lead exchange that involves more than one form of lead exchange is known as an **exchange of exchanges**, but before we get ahead of ourselves, let's talk about what these exchanges are:

Geographic Lead Exchanges: This model involves organizations who service areas in a **specific geographic area**. While technology does enable companies to provide services virtually everywhere, geography still plays a significant role for any customer acquisition strategy. For example, many companies have fiber networks that cover a specific region or building. It's also common for sales reps to be responsible for a **specific territory or vertical**. This specific model does not always work well for companies with a national footprint, but it's important to keep in mind that lead exchanges are made for individual relationships within organizations (not the entire company). Your lead exchange will allow you to align with the individual's geographical parameters/market, enabling you to form a geographical exchange with other territories. Even when your territory is the whole planet earth, you will find that your customer acquisition costs **will always go down if you stay local**. Once you run out of prospects in your market (after selling everyone your service) **then move on to the next city**.

The geographic lead exchange allows you to **focus** on

your area and pass along opportunities in other markets to fellow lead exchange members. For example, if you offer support to an office in your area, but need someone to service another office, you would lean on your lead exchange to support the client.

Vertical Lead Exchanges: Like geographic lead exchanges, this model is for companies and or reps who are disciplined enough to focus on a **specific vertical**. While there may not be a formal vertical assignment for you, it is wise to **narrow your focus**. Like geography, **the smaller your target, the smaller your acquisition costs will be**. There is nothing wrong with moving beyond our vertical focus, **but only after we dominate it**. If Amazon would have started selling everything in the beginning, they would end up selling nothing; instead, they **focused on books, conquered the space, and slowly moved into other areas of expertise**. Likewise, Facebook focused on the United States while Myspace reached for global dominance.

One of the primary advantages of a vertical lead exchange is that you can **coexist** with your lead exchange members in the **same** geographical market and still collaborate on opportunities. A slightly different but also common form of this lead exchange is working with individuals who work in the same vertical, but offer **complimentary products**. This is truly **the pinnacle of lead exchange groups**, enabling you to focus your efforts, stay local, and offer superior products from lead exchange members.

Product Lead Exchange: A product lead exchange leverages the most important element of the lead exchange model by having **complimentary products** that strengthen each other (the one-way street referral partnerships). This works well for individuals who need to avoid geographic constraints and need someone to partner with.

Sometimes these relationships can be tricky if your company offers every product under the sun. There may be a conflict of interest if you refer business to a lead exchange member that you could potentially sell inhouse. In the end you need to do **what's best for the client** and it will likely be a decision you make on a case-by-case basis. There needs to be enough skin in the game for everyone involved and it's something you will need to discuss with your employer and your lead exchange members. If you are exploring a product-based lead exchange, it's wise to create a hard rule that enables you to pass a particular line of business to your lead exchange members **without any question**.

Ideally what you want in a lead exchange is a small group of members who are **talking to the same clients**. An example of a lead exchange group would involve a bandwidth provider, SD-WAN provider, commercial real-estate agent, moving company, insurance broker, and a business consultant. In general, each member of the group would be interested in talking to the same clients and **often times are calling the same company**, but for **different reasons**.

Not everyone in the group is going to participate in every opportunity, but everyone will eventually win deals **overtime**. In order to ensure the success of the exchange, **money needs to be involved**. This will help **solidify** the commitment from the team members. A monthly **lead exchange fee** can be established, which will be used to fund **joint marketing campaigns**. An optimal means of financing the lead exchange funds is through referral fees. Rather than paying members of the exchange an override for referrals, use these incentives to finance the lead exchange fund.

The lead exchange has many built in advantages. When companies buy each other, one of the primary objectives is to create **related diversification** (when companies share resources to save money). The same concept applies here (just without the messy acquisition process). Individually you may not be able to afford a full-time marketing resource, but collectively you can hire a top-of-the-line marketing executive. There may be other resources you can pool together like accounting, IT, office space, events, software, licenses, and of course marketing campaigns. Because you are all targeting the same clients, the cost of acquiring customers will drop significantly.

In addition to combining your marketing dollars, you will also combine your sales efforts and **dedicate weekly time to outbound sales efforts**. If each member commits to three hours of outbound marketing efforts a day, you will end up with more outbound sales hours as a whole than you could accomplish on your own. **This is the ultimate advantage of working with referral partners** or a lead exchange; dividing up the burden of finding customers is **much easier as a team**. Natural incentives can be created from these campaigns. The more appointments you generate for others can be used to determine which company is focused on next.

As a team you will select a sales strategy (discussed later) and will execute it as a team. There will be a **score card**, enabling you to use **gamification** to keep everyone **accountable** (accountability is what differentiates referral partners from lead exchanges). It's recommended that the outbound campaigns focus on a different member each week. In the end multiple opportunities should stem from each deal **due to the synergistic nature of the products** each member represents. Strategizing together will enable you to achieve a **governance economy** (sharing knowledge for growth) to accelerate your success beyond your competition. To help solidify the team effort, **group rewards** and **goals** can be established, helping everyone to not only be united, but to **share success** secrets liberally.

It's always recommended that each member use their own money to participate in the exchange, but it's also very likely that there are vendor relationships that the members have who would be willing to pony up **marketing development funds**. Like your lead exchange members, the vendors you work with have a vested interest in your success and are usually willing if not desperately looking for somewhere to invest (we will talk about securing MDF funds in more detail later). Your lead exchange will significantly expand your access to MDF funds thanks to the number of vendors associated with each member of the team.

CHAPTER 3: LIST BUILDING

Once your referral partners have graduated to the level of a lead exchange, it's time to begin forming a sales strategy. Your group should focus on a **single strategy** in order to accurately **assess** everyone's performance. As a group you need to decide who your target audience will be.

An easy way to segment your target audience is based **on what they value**. If you focus on a vertical, but within the vertical companies have different expectations, **you will find it difficult to excel for each type of company**. Some businesses want white glove treatment while others want a simple solution just to get by. If your customer selection is disciplined, it's more likely customers will find and value you more.

Best Sources for B2B Sales Data:

- ZoomInfo
- Sales Intel
- Ensable
- Salesgenie
- Lead411
- Apollo

Here are a few of the top strategic list building strategies:

I. **Bad Reviews:** A great place to begin identifying potential clients is on **Google Maps**. Within Google Maps you can perform a search for any of your competitors and **publicly see their customer reviews**. Reviews provide not only detailed information about what your competitors **are doing well**, but what they're **doing wrong**. Google publishes the **full name** of the individual and or business who makes the comment, making it easy to compile a list of your competitor's customers (especially the ones who are dissatisfied with your competitor's service). It won't be hard to find the individual on LinkedIn using their name and location. Once you identify the individual, look the company up at: www.upsellreport.com

II. **Atlas Selling:** This strategy involves uncovering neighborhood contacts for your prospecting list. As we discussed in the referral partner chapter, **it is more effective to work with people that are local** than people that are the right contact in other markets. This particular strategy is known as **internal referrals**. When you engage your neighborhood contacts, **the close proximity** will provide you leverage, helping you find your way to the right individual. **Internal referrals are**

more effective than outside referrals or direct contacts due to the **social pressure** associated with responding to co-workers. Essentially when someone within the company (your neighbor) refers you to a decision maker, it forms a **social obligation** for them to respond **stronger** than almost any other contact method.

Simply **type your street name and city into the search box and names and addresses will begin to appear**. Once you identify your neighbors, you can add them on LinkedIn with a personalized message stating that you live in the neighborhood and wanted to connect. The initial message should not involve a request to talk to their IT manager, but it should be a friendly connection request. You will **need to build a**

relationship with these individuals before you ask for a favor.

The most effective relationship builder is **asking for favors**. When you run into a situation you truly need help with, **ask them for help**. As human beings **we love to help**. In times of disaster or need we find our **greatest strength** is revealed when we help others. This is part of our nature and is one of the fastest and strongest relationship builders. If you need help moving something or if you know someone that is looking for a job, these are perfect examples of how you can begin to connect and build relationships with your neighbors. It's also a great idea to connect and interact on www.nextdoor.com.

III. **Win Backs:** Another excellent source for prospecting lists are **past clients** also known as **win backs**. Not all companies keep track of this data or may be too new to have a vast list to work off of. Often times it is more effective to work with your **vendor relationships** to secure this type of list. Not all vendors are willing to share this with you, but if you build strong relationships of trust, you will find it easy to secure the list. When companies do demonstrate resistance, the best way to frame the request is in the **form of an experiment**. This is also a sales strategy that we will discuss later, but anything labeled as an experiment almost always **gets approved**. You simply have to explain to your vendor that you would like to help them recover these clients and you would like to run an experiment to see what type of results you will find. Ask for a list of 50 to 100 clients they have worked with in the past to run the experiment.

The primary reason you will find resistance in securing a win back lists is because people are afraid of looking bad in front of their peers. The experiment model allows you to remove any risk by saying that **it's ok to fail because it's an experiment**. Once they see this as an experiment, they have nothing to lose and everything to gain. It also enables the individual to **take the credit for the experiment** if it does go well.

It's not uncommon for the contacts at these companies to be out of date. Feel free to use LinkedIn or www.UpsellReport.com to **refresh any business contacts**. While it may feel daunting to reach out to a company you've never spoken to (especially when it's likely the contact isn't even there), it really is quite easy based on the fact that **there is a history with the company** via your vendor relationship. This single link **will help remove/reduce the fear of cold calling** and make outbound sales less painful.

Win back opportunities are not limited to only past customers, but can also apply to your vendors customer's **competitors, neighbors,** and **lost bids**. These last win back categories will require trust and strong relationships before they will share this data with you. It will be easier to access these types of lists if you are able to join their sales team as a **virtual sales rep**. It would also be helpful to combine the win back lists of your lead exchange group to expand your contact possibilities.

LinkedIn: A hybrid list approach would be related to an in-bound sales strategy that we will discuss later. Both your LinkedIn profile and website will experience inbound traffic. The individuals who visit your LinkedIn profile should be documented and added to your prospecting lists. Likewise, your website traffic should be documented using anonymous website trackers like www.leadforensics.com.

IV. **Named Lists:** is another great list strategy. This strategy focuses on a commonality that is unique to you as an individual: **your name**. If you go to LinkedIn and **find prospects with the same first or last name**, you can use this commonality to form an instant bond to help start a conversation. Tools like ancestery.com will also help you find distant cousins that can help you form lifelong relationships based on your common ancestry (especially if you take the DNA test).

The key element to any prospecting lists is finding a **soft connection** (like a win back, LinkedIn profile view, neighbor, etc.). This will not only **reduce the fear** element of outbound sales, but more importantly it will **change the attitude** of those making outbound sales to speak with **confidence** and authority rather than fear.

It's important to not overthink the list strategy. Sometimes we plan too far ahead and get caught up in the details. The best rule of thumb is the **look-then-leap principal.** Rather than meticulously going through each option, review **thirty-seven percent** of your options and **go with your favorite.**

CHAPTER 4: LINKEDIN

While LinkedIn is technically an appointment strategy, its strategic importance merits its own chapter within this book. LinkedIn has two primary purposes, **finding and being found**. The latter will be most important and will prove to be a valuable **inbound sales strategy** if executed correctly.

Inbound LinkedIn traffic is centered around your **personal brand** not your company's brand. In order to maximize your profile traffic, you must optimize your LinkedIn **search ranking** and significantly expand your profile **inroads**.

Due to the generic search box used in LinkedIn, the most important variable for ranking **is your name**.

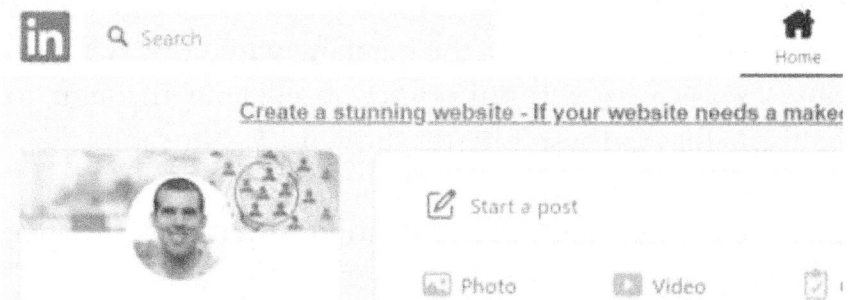

LinkedIn provides separate fields for your first and last name. Depending on the length of your name, it may be possible to use the first field for your first and last name.

The last name field can be used for a one or two keyword phrase you hope to rank for (like SD-WAN, UCaaS etc).

These same keywords can be used as your **custom profile URL** (this will help you rank within Google searches as well). A custom URL keyword is extremely valuable because you will leverage LinkedIn's amazing search engine ranking combined with your URL. For example rather than using: linkedin.com/in/justinchugg, you could try: linkedin.com/in/sd-wan-expert.

Within your profile there are two sections that reflect your title. The traditional formal title and your headline. Most profiles use their title in both, but the best profiles **change their headline to optimize their search ranking**. The headline is not only the second most important factor for search terms, but is also **critical for your click through rate**. You will need to balance how you describe yourself via the headline with your keyword phrases because without someone clicking through to your profile, it doesn't matter how well your rank.

Here are a few examples of headlines that would entice someone to click through to your profile:

- Helping Healthcare Providers Avoid Costly Mistakes
- Solving Healthcare's 3 Toughest Problems

- Unbiased Healthcare Advisor
- Solving the Top 10 Problems in Healthcare
- Giving Healthcare Providers 3 Hours Back a Day
- Helping Healthcare Providers Keep Their Clients
- Eliminating IT in Healthcare
- Implementing the Top 10 Trends in Healthcare
- Helping Save Healthcare Organizations
- Helping Healthcare Organizations Fire Unneeded Staff
- Undoing Bad Technology Decisions
- Retaining Healthcare Clients
- Using Technology to Avoid Healthcare Lawsuits
- Using Technology to Get Healthier Clients
- Enabling Patients to Show Up to Their Appointments
- Using Technology to Avoid HIPAA Violations
- Helping Others Recognize the Top 3 HIPAA Violations
- Top Three Reasons Doctors Go Out of Business

Your profile should in some way cater to and address the question/hook found in your headline. It's also helpful to use **keyword stuffing** (adding lots of keywords to your profile content) your profile in a way that helps you rank for a variety of keywords. There are potentially thousands of keywords you can add to your profile related to your industry. These should be buried in sections less visible/relevant to your prospect (like past job descriptions, schooling, keywords, etc.).

The most common mistake individuals make on their profile **is to talk about themselves**. Your prospects **are not interested in you** and how great you are, they're interested in understanding **how you can help them**. Anything else is **irrelevant** and will drive your prospects **away**. Below are two examples of contrasting profile summaries that will help illustrate this principal:

> *We are the leading technology adviser in Kansas City. Our clients have trusted us for more than 15 years with their technology decisions. We leverage the latest technologies to bring innovative, efficient communication solutions to businesses around the world.*

A better version would look like:

> *JFT Consulting helps **your** medical office provide seamless IT solutions without the need to hire/manage internal staff.*
>
> *As the **only** independent healthcare technology adviser in Kansas City, no one is better positioned to help **you** make the right decision about **your** technology solutions.*
>
> *With more than 15 years in the healthcare industry and hundreds of happy clients, JFT consulting knows what is going to work for **your** business. Call us today for a free consultation: (###) ###-####.*

As you describe your value proposition, it needs to have a clear quantitative value that caters directly to the prospect. Never forget to include a **phone number and or email;** this will help the prospect get a hold of you easier.

In addition to optimizing your keywords, it's important to create **commonalities**. There are two commonalities that will help your profile rank higher within LinkedIn: **common groups and common connections**.

To begin, identify prospects you would like to sell to. **Join the same LinkedIn groups as your prospects**. Once you list the top groups your prospects are members of, join the **largest ones first**. The larger ones will help you optimize the common ground you share with **more people**. LinkedIn groups also enable you to send **direct messages to anyone else within the same group**. On a side note, some groups can also help you identify **unique interest groups**. In one example a sales rep who enjoys creating amateur radio stations, found a group on LinkedIn full of people who shared this unique hobby. He was able to genuinely connect and share his passion with other group members, leading to long term relationships. Note it's important to identify groups with unique interests in order for them to be impactful.

In addition to increasing the common groups, you should also increase your **common connections**. Using the "connections of" filter in the search box for people, you will be able to identify the connections of your prospects by adding their name here plus a second-degree filter search results in the filters section. Increasing your common connections will enable your profile to outrank other profiles with equivalent keyword strategies.

When connecting to prospects, you may need to temporarily adjust your headline to incentivize prospects to accept your LinkedIn invites. Think about what's in it for them? How might they benefit from you connecting to them? Always include a custom invite text.

Richard van der Blom from "Just Connecting Hub" shared the ultimate connection formula on LinkedIn:

1. Review their recent posts
2. Send an invite based on a relevant post: Hey [FIRSTNAME], great to connect with you. Saw your recent post about [X] – totally agree. I had a similar experience with [Y] recently and noticed [your point of view]. Optional CTA: Just curious, have you considered doing [X] differently?

Not only is this conversation polite and to the point… You're also providing something to the prospect without asking for anything in return. You're asking meaningful questions that keep the conversation going. Try that in your next LinkedIn message.

When following up with a prospect, remember the optimal sequence is every four days.

Follow ups should use the following message strategy:
1. a noteworthy tip related to their field
2. a valuable tool they can incorporate into their work
3. a recommended resource for their use
4. an engaging quote or intriguing tidbit.

A great way to begin a follow up is: "I forgot to mention…"

Initial conversations should avoid using calendar tools to schedule appointments. This is too forward and will burn the relationship bridge with the prospect. These tools are extremely useful when the time is right, but not in the initial conversation.

Pattern Interrupt: Capture a screenshot of their logo or any of the following: Locate a video featuring them and take a screenshot; visit their blog page; explore their volunteer section and capture a screenshot; inquire if they attended the same university; delve into their location, hobbies, and shared work history.

Pose Irresistible Yes-or-No Questions: Avoid complex queries to facilitate quick responses.
A. Admire your logo; did you create it?

B. Impressed by your YouTube presence; have you always been camera-confident?
C. Enjoyed your recent blog post; can we expect more soon?
D. Aim to convey your genuine interest in them.

If a prospect ignores your invite, you can uninvite them via LinkedIn and retry a few months later.

To bypass the standard LinkedIn invite limits, you can add prospect's emails to a Gmail account, integrate the Gmail account with LinkedIn and allow LinkedIn to invite the prospects for you.

Common connections will also enable you to focus on a group of prospects that share the same realm of expertise, enabling you to build your expertise in their space. Becoming an expert is a fast and easy shortcut to driving **inbound traffic**. The stronger your expertise in a focused area, the stronger the triggers will be in your prospect's mind to think of you. For instance, if you focus on technology, your friends may or may not remember you. If you focus on technology for fast food restaurants, it will engender a stronger trigger for people when they encounter someone in that space. Connecting with individuals within a specific vertical on LinkedIn will increase the common connections and your ranking.

Your profile will also see a significant traffic boost by listing your vendor relationships. This is not a generic list you provide in your summary section, but would be found **in your employment section**. If you have strategic vendor relationships, you can legitimately list yourself as a solution provider, business partner, etc. for that specific company. This will enable your profile to appear when prospects are searching for **contacts within that organization**.

In addition to improving your search ranking, creating **inroads** will further **augment your profile's view count. An inroad is considered a link back to your profile**. To start your LinkedIn profile link needs to be embedded in your email signature. You may not always be able to see who hits your website, but you can identify individuals who go to your LinkedIn profile.

Within LinkedIn there are a large number of inroad possibilities. To begin you can **follow companies** and **LinkedIn profiles**. Individual follows will not amount to much, but **collectively they will**. Individuals who see the followers of an organization/individual will see your profile, leading to clicks from time to time. With enough follows, you will be able to drive a steady flow of traffic **back to your profile**.

Another inroad involves clicking on your prospect's profiles so that you show up in the list of **individuals looking at their profile**. Ideally you should click on one-hundred profiles a day. It's important that you **enable your profile to be visible** when you click on other profiles via your privacy settings (see below).

Visibility of your profile & network
Make your profile and contact info only visible to those you choose

Profile viewing options — Change
Choose whether you're visible or viewing in private mode

Story viewing options — Change
Choose whether you're visible or viewing in private mode

Edit your public profile — Change
Choose how your profile appears to non-logged in members via search

Who can see or download your email address — Change
Choose who can see your email address on your profile and in approved apps or download it in their data export

If you are in sales, it's **recommended** that you turn on all public visibility settings, enabling your profile to not only be more visible across LinkedIn, but Google as well. When planning ahead, you can click on the profiles of the companies you plan on calling/emailing in the upcoming weeks so that your name and face feel familiar to them.

When viewing other profiles, you will notice a list of suggested profiles on the right. There are two ways to encourage LinkedIn to recommend your profile in their algorithm: **recommendations** and **projects**. When you recommend someone, it creates a **permanent gateway between your profile and the other profile**; hopefully the recommendation will be reciprocated further cementing the profile relationships. Projects are a feature within LinkedIn which enables you to share details about projects you have participated in with other individuals. This will likewise create a **two-way link between you and other profiles**. Even if the LinkedIn does not feature you as a related profile, there will still be a **link back to your profile**, helping once again increase the number of **inroads** back to you.

A more manual, but meaningful exercise is interactions. Birthdays, work anniversaries, posts, and other significant posts, provide ample opportunity for you to engage and build relationships in a **natural way**. When extending birthday wishes and congratulations, it is helpful to **wait until after the event** to avoid getting lost in the mass communications. This should go without saying, but the communications should be unique, meaningful, and encourage responses. For example, if it's a work anniversary you may say something like: **Wow 8 years that's incredible! Your employer must really love you. I would love to catch up soon. Please let me know when you're in town again. I know a great Brazilian restaurant here you should check out.**

Work anniversaries and birthdays do not allow the level of frequency you need to maintain with prospects in order to always stay in front of the client. It's wise to direct message your LinkedIn connections **every six weeks** or so to maintain your momentum. The messages should be more than "just checking in". Your most effective messages will ask your connections about their

opinion. Not only will this **flatter them**, but encourage them to engage and share information (more about this later). Each profile visit should also include a skill endorsement, which is another great way to grab their attention.

Managing LinkedIn can be a lot of work, but can also be an ideal opportunity for an **intern**. If you can't find an intern, look for executive assistants on Upwork. Either of two can help eliminate a lot of the manual labor associated with building LinkedIn momentum without having to invest too much time.

LinkedIn should be your starting point with any prospect. Emails and phone calls are not only invasive, but feel **desperate**. LinkedIn is a **less threatening** more natural way to engage and build relationships with prospects. It's important to not overwhelm your prospects in the beginning. If you treat your LinkedIn connections as prospects, it will be as if you never connected with the individual. You need to treat them like a friend, asking for **advice**, giving advice, and ultimately **finding ways to help each other**.

The primary purpose of all these exercises is to **drive traffic to your LinkedIn profile**. You will need a premium LinkedIn profile to gain full visibility into everyone who is clicking on your profile, but if you use this strategy, it will be well worth it. Never wait longer than a day to follow up with prospects who view your profile; otherwise, they will forget you. When you reach out, **ask what they might have been looking for**. Always suggest you meet sometime in the future. Anyone and everyone who views your profile **should be added to your prospecting list** and cadence (if you chose to communicate with prospects on a regular basis). It may feel like a lot of work to generate inbound LinkedIn leads, but it is a lot less expensive than generating outbound sales strategies. To keep tabs on an individual and or company try the following tool: ensable.com/follow or google.com/alerts.

Another powerful strategy to drive relevant traffic to your personal LinkedIn profile consists of searching for hashtags on LinkedIn (like: #Insurance) and interacting with these posts. If you are a set up as an admin for your company, you can likewise comment/like on behalf of the company. It is recommended to limit the daily interactions to around 700 per day (although this number can change based on how LinkedIn changes it's policies).

As you develop your LinkedIn network and company pages, it's important to reach your audience through posts and interactions. One factor that will significantly influence your ability to get in front of your peers is LinkedIn's algorithm. A prominent social media consultant, **Richard Van Der Blom** (linkedin.com/in/richardvanderblom), spent more than over 1,200 hours researching LinkedIn's algorithm to better understand how LinkedIn decides whether to prioritize your traffic:

- Only publish once every 18 hours. Each additional post will reduce your visibility by 15%
- If a post receives interactions (comments/likes) within the first 90 minutes, will significantly perpetuate the long-term success and engagement of the post.
- Posts that involve "selfies" will generate 3x more engagement and 2.5x more reach.
- The optimal post text should be between 1,200 to 1,600 characters.
- If you engage with at least 3 other posts immediately after publishing your own post, you will see a 20% uplift on your original posts reach.
- The optimal posting times vary by day and should generally meet this schedule:
    - Monday 10AM - 1 PM
    - Tuesday 8 AM - 11AM
    - Wed 9AM - 11AM
    - Thu 8AM - 11AM
    - Fri 1PM - 3PM
    - Sat 10AM - 1PM
- Avoid editing a post within the first 10 minutes of publishing. (Reduces reach by 10 to 40 percent)
- Resist the temptation to be the first one to comment on your post. This will reduce your reach by 20%.

- LinkedIn offers a variety of post styles. Each type of post yields a different return on reach. Here are a few examples of which posts yield the highest results:
    - Selfies (3x)
    - Document Post (2.2x to 3.4x)
    - Polls (2.1 to 2.9x)
    - Carousel Post (1.8x to 2.3x)
    - Text + Multiple Pics (1.2x to 1.6x))
    - Videos (0.5x to 0.8x)
    - Posts with 1 external link (0.4 to 0.5x)
    - Posts with 2+ external links (0.2 to 0.4x) (note if you need to include an external link, edit the post one hour after you publish it as a comment).
- Including a selfie in your post slides will increase reach by 80 to 90 percent.
- Polls have become very popular on LinkedIn. The optimal poll should include 2 questions. The optimal duration of a poll is one week. Running a poll for two weeks will generate more views, but less votes per 1,000 views.
- When publishing videos on LinkedIn, consider using the following techniques:
    - Captioned videos outperform non captioned videos by 35% on reach and 25% on engagement
    - Use a native video (upload to LinkedIn)
    - Use Square Format

- o Videos where you play the lead role will yield better results compared to videos with other people (-40%) or that have no people in it at all (-75%)
- Posts should use **three hashtags**. If you use more or less, it will reduce your reach.
- Remember it is important that others comment first on your post, but in order to increase your posts visibility, you need to reply to all comments in the first hour after publishing. Your post will experience a 20% growth for each comment and will grow an additional 4% within your own network, and 3% in the network of the person that commented. Adding multiple comments (2-4) as an author, after 24 hours, will relaunch the post in the feed of all contributors, leading to +25% extra growth.
- If you are a creator (minimum two posts a week), and stop posting for more than a month, the first 4 to 5 posts will receive about 30% less reach than before.
- Tagging yourself in the original post does not impact your reach or engagement.

CHAPTER 5: GETTING APPOINTMENTS

In our last chapter we explored one of the most effective sales strategies on LinkedIn. Each of the following strategies should **complement LinkedIn (not replace it)**. Ideally you want to explore two strategies simultaneously. At the end of each month the less effective strategy should be replaced with an alternative initiative. Sales will always be a **moving target** and constantly comparing new strategies will enable you to stay relevant in a noisy world.

The following strategies outline potential experiments you can run to see what works best for you:

1. **Group Purchasing Sales:** Throughout this book we have recommended specializing as a means to lower your customer acquisition costs. Group purchasing is a strategy that will reward you tremendously for having a **disciplined prospecting group**. Group purchasing enables you to truly execute a blue ocean strategy (lower costs + differentiation).

    The basics behind a group purchasing model is **pre-negotiating discounted rates for a common group of companies and or**

individuals. Many of these groups exist today. It functions similar to a union that leverages the strength of the group rather than the individual. This is an extremely effective means of acquiring and keeping customers. The discounted rates will need to be negotiated with your employer and or vendors.

You will find it easier to work with smaller vendors (as they are more flexible) to create these strategic relationships. If they are resistant, use the experimental approach and recommend that you try it out on a small group of companies.

Rather than try to explain how this would work, it will be easier to provide an example to illustrate this model. Let's say you're interested in selling to small dental offices across the United States. You would create a website that houses the dental office's group information. The best purchasing groups will charge a **membership fee**. Within the industry you're catering to, it needs to be small enough to help the members **feel exclusive**. You will need to identify everything these organizations **purchase**. Whether it's toothbrushes, fluoride, phone service, internet, etc. List all vendors who supply these materials. Once you have the company list, run it through www.upsellreport.com to identify the appropriate contacts at these organizations. Before you blast your entire list with emails, it's important to have a few strategic vendors lined up first. This will help new vendors feel the urgency to get on the bandwagon. It's recommended that you likewise charge your vendors for a membership fee and allow them to compete for a position within the group by offering **deeper discounts**. Limit the number of vendors who will participate.

Your website should outline the vendors you work with. It's important to negotiate with vendors the ability to lower an existing customer's rates if they work with you. If they are not flexible, simply recommend to the client that they use an alternative vendor to help put pressure on your vendors.

Your group purchasing network is a valuable asset. If you create this while you're employed, it will likely become the property of your employer. If you create these in-between jobs, it will be easier to use it as an **asset you can take with you to your next job interview**. You may need to consult with human resources and or a lawyer to help safeguard the ownership of your purchasing group.

The most valuable purchasing groups offer more than just discounts. As mentioned earlier in the lead exchange section, you should encourage members to refer business **to each other**, share **advice**, and host discussion boards to address hot topics. **Surveys** can provide valuable insights that are not visible within individuals, but found only by understanding everyone as a whole.

You will find that adding and keeping clients under this model will be much easier compared to traditional models. You will not only gain leverage over your vendors, but create a strategic price and value not found anywhere else. Your clients will be happier and your vendors will value your relationship and the influence you hold over the clients.

Email Template:
Subject: What do you think?
Email Body: I am forming a purchasing group here locally for #industry#. Do you have any vendors you could recommend?

Email Strategy: Here we want to involve the client and see if the vendor they recommend is already part of your network; if not, you can ask for their help to introduce you to someone at the company. The more they are involved, the more ownership and interest they will have in the purchasing group. If the vendor they recommend is already a member, it will be an easy way to discuss discounts and advantages of using the purchasing group.

2. **Negative Campaigns:** If you're struggling to grab a prospect's attention, you may need to become more **pessimistic**. Prospects are more inclined to learn from other's mistakes than other's triumphs. If you focus on campaigns that highlight what you don't like, you will garnish **more attention**.

    A few examples include:
    - Why I don't like...
    - 10 Things I Hate About...
    - Top Reasons Why I Switched...
    - Top 10 Worst Providers...
    - Most Expensive Vendors...

    Some of these examples/lists can be based on surveys, rankings from Google Maps, case studies, and just raw data. If you're using an **opinion sales** strategy, you can ask prospects which vendors they recommend and form a **net promoter score**. Technology vendor data can also be found on websites like **downdetector.com** helping identify the number and depth of outages they have experienced over the years. Providing a regular monthly and or quarterly report (via a **sideways sales letter**) highlighting the worst providers in an industry will certainly gain a lot more attention than highlighting the top vendors. It would still be worthwhile to provide a recommended vendor list as an alternative, but your traction will come from helping buyers know what to **avoid**.

You will likely get push back from the vendors who appear on the list. It's important that you stay neutral and base your data on facts and surveys to avoid any repercussions. It may be helpful to combine multiple data points to provide a more rounded approach.

Email Template:
Subject: Worst UCaaS Providers
Email Body: I thought you might appreciate a heads up on what's happening in the voice industry in case you need to switch providers in the future. I have surveyed companies here locally to see what their opinion is about different UCaaS providers. Here are the companies with the lowest rating:

1. Provider 1
2. Provider 2
3. Provider 3
4. Provider 4

Email Strategy: You'll notice there isn't a call to action here. In order to establish credibility, you need to simply provide information. As time goes on, you can continue to supply updates/insights (maybe replying to the same email string) and wait for the prospect to "ask" for recommendations.

In fact, leaving the top providers out of the email may end up being your **best strategy**. Any good sales strategy provides an incentive for the client to "ask" rather than "respond".

3. **Grant Sales:** Response rates are found to be 37% higher when the information discussed is less than twenty-four hours old. Finding new and relevant information every twenty-four hours can be challenging. One powerful solution to staying engaged with prospects is using grants. Everyday new business grants become available at: grants.gov, which creates a unique relevant and especially time sensitive information that will open doors to future prospects.

   The strategy is designed to drive inbound traffic to your website. By recreating an information page on your website with additional grant details, you can send prospects to your site to help them learn about the grant opportunity.

   It's helpful to implement a subdomain to your website, enabling you to create an entire parallel site that reflects your original content with a specific focus on the industry you're catering to. By doing so it will be much easier to convert inbound traffic to your site. By tracking visitors, you can follow up with prospects based on the pages they visit.

Email Template:
<u>Subject</u>: *New Business Grant*
<u>Email Body</u>: *I wanted to share with you a new grant that came out this morning for assessing risk epidemiologically. I don't know if you have the bandwidth to take on a project like this, but thought you should know about it.*

<u>Email Strategy</u>: The ultimate goal behind this email is to drive traffic to your site. The website needs to be optimized to not only keep your audience engaged, but also to convert your traffic into sales.

4. **Survey Sales:** Most reps don't realize this, but their biggest competitor is **Google**. Prospects turn to Google to find their next product. **If you can't offer information that doesn't already exist in Google, then you can't provide enough value to your prospects**. One of the most powerful sales tools is a **survey**. In general customers do not want to be sold to, so leading with a product offering will normally **raise** your customer acquisition costs. Surveys on the other hand cater to the customer's ego by **asking their opinion** about something. Not only does it make customer engagements **easier**, but it enables you to hold a **monopoly** on the valuable insights you learn from the surveys.

The most common question associated with surveys is how to I convince people to take the survey? The first strategy is using an Amazon gift card. You will be amazed what people will do for a $15 gift card, but the **greatest incentive** will be the **data** you collect (survey results). As part of our human nature, we are always **comparing ourselves** to others. It's our way of ensuring our survival because if everyone else is doing it, it must be **safe**. It's always a good idea to try both methods and possibly partner with vendors or lead exchange members to finance the gift cards (using marketing development funds).

Your discoveries will provide you with the perfect excuse to follow-up and thank your prospects for their time. It would also be wise to write about what you discovered. In order to induce interest in your audience and gather responses, it will be essential that the questions are relevant enough. Rather than leading with questions that relate to the products you sell, **focus on things that are top of mind for your clients**. What is the number one question they have? It's more important to find the answer to this question than anything else.

In one example a survey asked a group of companies what their number one challenge was. The primary response showed that they had insufficient parking for their employees. As a result, the sales rep developed a plan to enable workers to work remotely to help alleviate the problem. Another example of a good survey question that asked a group of hotels how they're competing with Airbnb. The answer will almost always reveal a strategy or an experiment that can help address the challenge.

Surveys will also work best when they deal with **"super trends"**. A super trend is anything that will have massive impact on society in the future (healthcare, global warming, crime, etc.). These types of questions combined with relevant industry questions will peak the interest the most with your audience.

Surveys should not consist of more than three questions. Additional information should be gathered automatically (business demographics, contact information etc.) using research and smart survey tools (like Google). When you invite someone via email through a Google form, it has the ability to capture their email automatically (just make sure you **test it before you execute the invite**).

Sometimes it helps to add some details to your survey results. The data by itself can be helpful, but a great excuse to follow-up with your survey helpers is to ask why they think the results are the way they are. This will help you prepare valuable articles to publish for your group.

Information collected can be converted into **virtual sales reps** by publishing articles outlining the information. Not only will this help you gain free advertising, but significant credibility when speaking with clients. Surveys should have a **cadence**, constantly trying to better understand the questions and the answers to an industry's biggest challenges.

Email Template:
Subject: Thoughts?
Email Body: I noticed you have a lot of experience in the hotel industry and wanted to get our opinion about something. Do you think the government needs to get involved in breaking up monopolies for internet pricing sites?

Email Strategy: It's important that your email goes right to the point. It's a common mistake with emailing for individuals to introduce themselves. The first sentence almost always needs to focus on the prospect to engage them. In this case we complimented their experience in the hotel industry, which fed their ego and kept them engaged. We also discussed a topic that may be sensitive and almost guaranteed to generate strong **emotions**. If it doesn't evoke a strong positive or negative emotion, you will **lose their attention.**

5. **Research & Experimentation Credits:** The government recognizes the value of smarter companies. To help encourage progress, the government instituted the 26 U.S.C. § 41 in 1981. The R&D credit rewards businesses for investing in **experiments** and **research** that improve **efficiency.** Regardless of the outcome of the experiments, the time and resources invested will be offset using this **credit.**

   With the right documentation, the tax credit is available to current and **past** tax years. The credit can be made available to the following scenarios:

   1) Advancements in **performance** reliability, or **process**
   2) Research and experimentation

   What expenses qualify?

   a. Utility and supply costs
   b. Wages of those involved
   c. 65%-100% of contract research expenses
   d. **Cloud computing** services

   If our products and services do not qualify for the R&D credit, we're doing something **wrong.** We need to truly understand the efficiency **impact** our services offer. This is the primary responsibility of the sales rep. If you cannot offer a **calculable** impact on their business, you need to do some homework (this is why we run experiments).

Rather than trying to manage the accounting and tax laws yourself, add an accounting and business consultant to your **lead exchange**. Keep in mind that the tax credit will be available **independent** of the success of the experiment. By properly **documenting** and using this tax credit, the government will help **finance** your product's impact and help you **discover** new possibilities and applications for your solution.

Email Template:
Subject: *Tax Credit*
Email Body: *Has your business taken advantage of the R&D tax credit? I was wondering if we could run an experiment with your company that could find new ROI and would be financed through the R&D tax credit.*

Can we jump on a quick call to discuss?

Email Strategy: You don't want to give too much information up front, but just enough to generate interest in a conversation. These emails are best targeted towards finance and executive departments. Once an appointment is booked, you need to be ready with a solid plan and overview of how to make this work. If you don't have a clear path, your client is going to get cold feet.

6. **Petitions:** Along a similar vein is the petition strategy. When verticals or markets experience a common enemy or challenge, petitions for change can drive strong response rates. The petition can not only provide one of your strongest response rates, but uncover challenges that will lead to sales. This should never be a one-time engagement but a fluid ongoing conversation about the topic and advances/changes related to it. You may find this to work well within a purchasing group.

Email Template:
Subject: *New Parking Laws*
Email Body: *Lately businesses are struggling due to a lack of parking. I am creating a petition to provide new parking for businesses in this area at the vacant lot next to main street.*

Would you be willing to sign this please?

Email Strategy: It's not hard to get a response here, but it may be more challenging to translate these responses into sales. Independent of whether there is a direct correlation between the petition and future sales, the conversation will ultimately lead to relationships and relationships will lead to future sales.

7. **Customer Customer Sales:** The value of your product is not intrinsic; it has to be **discovered**. In addition to uncovering challenges by surveying your customers, a deeper level of value can be found by understanding your customer's **customers**. Nearly every new product requires adapting and significant change, not to mention the inherent risk of the unknown. To offset this cost, the value must be **disproportionally** larger than the cost.

The only way to create this value is through a better understanding of the application of the product or service (outcome). As you better understand the values and challenges your customer's customers face, the value of your product will begin to **crystalize** and you will begin to form a monopoly within the space you're catering to. This monopoly will exist because you will have a unique understanding of their business.

Here are a few questions you may consider using to understand your customer's customers:

- Why did you chose this company?
- Why did you stop using another company?

- What do you like about their service?
- What do you not like about their service?
- How did you find them?
- Have you considered outsourcing this job?

You can find the answers to these questions without having to speak to anyone by looking at **Google reviews**. It would be valuable to talk to as many clients as you can to get additional insights not found on Google reviews.

Your customer's customers often times have a choice about whether to hire internally or outsource the job to your customer's business. Surveying companies who have decided to hire internally can also be a valuable source of information for your client. Because we live in a time of customer empowerment, the most common solution to challenges will be related to better customer service. Regardless of the problem, it's necessary to explore how your product will solve any gaps you uncover with their clients.

The solution and the problem are two very different things. Rather than assuming you know what to do, always approach the problem with an experiment and ask your clients if they would be willing to try a few ideas to address the challenges you have uncovered.

Email Template:
<u>Subject</u>: *Customer Feedback*
<u>Email Body</u>: *I recently gathered some interesting insights after interviewing clients from the glass industry and wanted to share some insights with you.*

Attached is a copy of what I learned from my discussions with these clients.

<u>Email Strategy</u>: While it's tempting to try to discuss products and sales, it's usually a little too early in the sales cycle to bring this up with this model. At this point you want to establish yourself as an authority. You also want to generate a reply. If your client thinks this is going to be a sales discussion, they will be less reluctant to reply. Here you need to simply share and wait. If and when they reply, you can begin discussing other insights and solutions you have found related to your discoveries. After establishing a relationship, you may ask the client if they would be willing to try an **experiment** related to the insights.

8. **Experimental Sales:** Surveys more often than not answer the what, **but not the how**. If you are lucky enough to uncover the problem, finding the solution is **exponentially more valuable**. Experimental sales will not only **grease the wheels on any sales conversation**, but allow you

to discover one of the most powerful **sales monopolies** ever.

An experimental sale is not very different from a traditional sale. The difference is primarily in **the approach**. Rather than asking your client to take a risk with a new service, you invite the prospect to run an experiment. Explore the ROI possibilities, see what type of impact this will have. This is easiest when combined with surveys, because the **surveys help uncover the problems and the experiments attempt to solve the problem.**

For example, if dental offices share that their biggest challenge is missed appointments, an experimental sale would ask a number of dental offices to test drive a new texting services that integrates with their customer appointment setting tool. Run the experiment for a month and compare the results. **Regardless of the outcome, your audience will be interested to know what you find**. This is a great way to maintain a cadence with your survey audience.

Experimental sales create one of the most powerful messaging tools available to you. As you begin to discover what works and what doesn't, new solutions will begin to emerge. **Stories are and always will be the most effective means of**

communicating your message. Not only does it **captivate** your audience, but it provides a level of understanding not found anywhere else. The **context** of the story not only enables a better understanding of your value, but creates a long-term remembrance of the value due to the **emotional impact** it brings. It's just as important to include how you reached your conclusion as the conclusion itself.

While nearly all viral content has a story, not all stories are viral. In order to engineer viral content, there are a few things to consider: First, your story needs to **evoke strong emotions.** If your audience does not experience an emotional reaction to your story, it will reach a dead end. The emotional reaction encourages your audience to share the content in order to form an emotional bond with other likeminded individuals (experiencing the same emotions creates a higher level of connectedness). The content should enable your audience to **better define themselves to others.** If your content enables others to help themselves look smarter, feel kinder, or cooler, it will **increase** the likelihood of them sharing your content. Using the example of the dental office, talk about their struggles, their dreams and why they opened the business. Discuss the impact the experiment had on their business and how it helps them help others. Every piece of good content will become a virtual sales rep for your organization. Never under estimate the value of good content as it almost always is less expensive and more effective than a full-time sales representative.

The experience learned from the experiment will provide instant value to those who read/watch what you share. **Because people like to help others, this will be one of the primary factors driving the viral aspect of the content related to your discoveries.** Keep in mind that people are more interested in what **not to do** than what they should do. This is due to the fact that as humans we are more interested in **avoiding mistakes** than we are in seeking success. For this reason, always remember to share your failures and your successes.

Many of your vendor relationships offer free-trials. If they don't, usually you can convince them to offer a month-to-month contract to exemplify the value of the experiment. If you find success, it won't be hard to celebrate together using **marketing development funds** to spread the good news. Remember to employ video and engage **industry magazines** to share your discovery. You will often find that your audiences will be more interested in the failures than the triumphs. This mindset (also known as an antifragile mindset) is evident with a plane crash. Everyone wants to know why. Antifragility (the ability to learn from mistakes) enables optionality. Optionality enables you to make good decisions without innate intelligence. You simply need to recognize what works and what doesn't and follow the path (asymmetry + rationality).

To execute a successful optionality strategy, you must be open to change. Your goals need to be fixed, but general; while your tactics need to be specific, but flexible.

The successes on the other hand will generate what Collins in "Good to Great" calls the **"Flywheel"**. Every positive decision should and will reinforce your **hedgehog** (specialization) competencies. Becoming a hedgehog is the **epitome of transitioning from good to great**. When you run an experiment, you don't need to worry about finding your specialization because **your specialization will find you based on the positive outcomes** associated with your experiments.

Email Template:
Subject: *Crazy Idea*
Email Body: *I wanted to run an idea by you.*

I've noticed that a lot of people cancel appointments in your industry. What if we tested a video appointment system to see if people would keep their appointments more (since they don't have to drive to your office)?

Would you be willing to test this idea?

Email Strategy: If you have done your homework on a specific business/vertical, it shouldn't be hard to come up with a strategy that would interest your client. You don't need to explain everything in the first email. In fact, less information is better because you want them to ask for more information.

9. **Book Publishing**: Writing a book normally isn't the first thing you think of when you consider your next sales strategy, **but it should be**. In the age of self-publishing, creating a book is easier than ever. Rather than explain all the details, I would recommend googling how to publish your first book on YouTube and find the latest and greatest information there.

Book Publishing will help you **change your perception with prospects more than anything else**. Becoming an author creates a **coat of influence**. Competence and brilliance **are not self-evident**. It can take a long time to earn someone's trust (it may be longer than the sales cycle). A book becomes the equivalent of a doctor's coat, which helps provide **instant credibility**.

Writing a book can be much easier than you think. If you plan ahead, it can be done before you start. As we mentioned before, the articles you publish outlining your survey and experiment studies will serve as chapters in your book. You may need to make some modifications, but in general the content will already exist if you think ahead. Try to create the storyline ahead of time as you plan your surveys and experiments.

In addition to helping, you achieve authority status, book writing is also one of the greatest door openers **of all time**. When you have a hard time reaching a high-level executive, **invite them to a book interview**. This approach will again cater to their ego and allow you direct access to some of the hardest to reach executives. Ask for their insights about the experiments and surveys you are running.

Books are especially valuable in a market where the relationship between price and value is eroding due to the nearly free marketplace for online information. In his book "Free" Anderson suggests that **price takes a backseat to "reputation" and "attention"**. In order to compete in an era that looks beyond pricing will require you to become a publisher and earn your prospect's business with the **currency of reputation and attention.**

Once your book is published, by using Amazon, it's easy to distribute your book to prospects via the Kindle gifting tool. By placing your book at the lowest price possible ($0.99), it will be cost effective to send the book virtually to as many prospects as you want (999 at a time). When sending books, a generous messaging text field is provided by Amazon allowing you to create a custom message for your audience. Essentially it becomes a very cost-effective email tool.

Email Template:
Subject: Interview
Email Body: *I'm writing a book about the hotel industry and wanted to see if I could interview you about something. Do you have a few minutes to chat?*

Email Strategy: You will notice the email is short. The content itself is enough to get a response, so no additional content is needed at this point. In fact, when you can get a response with less text, you will likely have a much more successful campaign. In almost any email campaign, the initial goal is not the sale (not yet at least), it's to get a response. The response will create a social obligation to continue the dialogue (it's easy ignore an email you haven't replied to, but not after you started a conversation).

10. **Opinion Sales**: In a similar but different approach, opinion sales can be an alternative/complimentary means of accomplishing survey strategies. The difference is that opinion sales **is less formal** and acts **more as an excuse to contact someone** rather than collecting information. Data can and should be collected, but the communication **should feel more natural to the prospect**. No one has ever wanted to be sold to (this is truer today than ever). When you sell something, it's all about you; where opinion selling is all about the prospect.

This particular strategy is normally employed on LinkedIn (as part of your communication cadence), but can be executed over the phone, email, or any other means.

Typically, we are asking an open-ended question about something new and relevant. We hope the prospect responds with: I haven't used this technology/product before, but I want to. Compiling a list of answers can also serve as a great white paper. Creating valid excuses to follow up with your prospects are golden opportunities. If you decide to publish a white paper with responses, ask permission to mention their name as an excuse to follow up. If they don't feel comfortable having their name on the page, ask if you can leave it anonymous.

Opinion based sales aligns with Collin's advice in the book Good to Great on how to generate awareness: 1) Lead with questions, not answers; 2) Engage in dialogue and debate, not coercion; 3) Conduct autopsies without blame; and 4) Build red flag mechanisms that turn information into information that cannot be ignored.

Email Template:
<u>Subject</u>: *Random question for you*
<u>Email Body</u>: *I'm doing some research on cloud-based firewalls and wanted to see if you have any experience in this area. Do you have any vendors you can recommend?*

<u>Email Strategy</u>: Because you will likely be reaching out to people your connected to on LinkedIn, there isn't a lot of need for introductions. Often times emails will start with: "I hope you're doing well" or "It's been a little while", etc. While it is nice to start emails with a little introduction, it's not necessary. Simple dialogues few more real and more natural, which is key to this strategy.

11. **Door to Door Sales**: Sometimes it makes sense to engage prospects face to face. Door to door prospecting can be challenging, but rewarding at

the same time. A more effective strategy involves meeting your clients face to face, but asking them to line up to meet you.

To generate a line of prospects, you will need to do some homework first. To begin you need to focus on multi-tenant buildings or a business park with a large quantity of tenants (30+). You can search for buildings by tenant count at: ensable.com/data.

Once you have a list of prospects, engage a few local food trucks (hopefully they are already in the area). It would make sense to negotiate a bulk discount on their services. You may also consider using members of your lead exchange to finance the opportunity. Using a postcard service, send a postcard to your ideal contacts for each building tenant inviting them to a free food truck meal on you.

The postcard will be used as a meal ticket. As your prospects line up for their meal, take advantage of the opportunity to introduce yourself and explain your services.

The strategy is best executed by emailing before and after the event. By establishing a relationship with the food truck owner, you may consider offering an advertising incentive (monthly rate/commissions) for placing an add on their truck.

Email Template:
Subject: Lunch?
Email Body: I wanted to check to see if you got my lunch invite for March 18th. It should have come in the mail. We are celebrating new fiber service at your building and inviting everyone to come down and enjoy a free meal (just bring your postcard)

Email Strategy: Nothing makes cold email easier than content that feels unique to the individual. In this strategy we are discussing a specific meeting (outside their building) and inviting them to lunch. A physical postcard has gone out, making it even more relevant. The combination of postcards, lunch, and emails, will produce a much higher response rate compared to traditional campaigns.

12. **Advertising**: While there are many advertising platforms available, there is a common underlying purpose behind advertising. In a way, advertising is like a **sideways sales letter** designed to **incrementally** change your audience's mindset. These marginal differences will help influence the buyer's decision when it comes time to buy. For this reason, we cannot always expect or correlate sales directly to advertising. **Advertising is more of an education system** than a lead funnel. In

most cases your prospect **is not ready to buy** when they see your ad. If you focus on persuading rather than click through rates, your prospect will be **more inclined to call you when the timing is right**; otherwise, you will be catering to the few that actually need your service now and missing out on the majority **who need your service in the future**.

Ads that employ the **Ogilvy layout principle** (also known as the two-thirds/one-third principle) will enjoy more success (70% more visibility). To use this strategy, the **top two-thirds** of an ad should be a **picture**. The bottom third should have a headline and below the headline a smaller font with additional details. The **Guillotine** principle suggests that the most effective pictures are **faces** (looking at you) and the most effective face pictures are **babies** (you may have to get creative to find ways to incorporate babies into your business ads).

13. **Sideways Sales Letter**: It's not uncommon that your messaging is **larger than your prospect's attention span**. A sideways sales letter is the most effective means of communicating your company's value proposition in a way that will **comprehensively be comprehended** by your prospects and clients.

A sideways sales letter is an **ongoing communication** that shares your values **little by little** bit by bit overtime, allowing your prospects to grasp and understand your value **one email at a time**.

Sideways sales letters are only effective **if your audience actually reads them**. In order to keep an audience engaged, your messaging must become a **trojan horse**. The case studies, the surveys, the experiments will all exemplify your value proposition indirectly while at the same time **entertaining your audience with new information**.

The purpose of every article **is to modify your prospect's perspective**. Start with the facts that your audience is willing to accept. Help your audience identify the problem your solution solves. When you reach facts that will contradict your prospect's beliefs, state their belief and **carefully** explain why it is wrong. If you can clearly explain the benefits of using your product on day one, it will be easier to convey its value. You are most likely to achieve change when you can **share information the user has not considered**. These types of changes come via insights born in the subconscious thought. **Questions that go beyond the superficial conscious mind will penetrate the** subconscious only when the answer to your questions <u>cannot immediately be found</u>. For example, you may ask: Would your business grow faster or slower by outsourcing some of your talent?

While logic has its place in convincing our audience, the era of **abundant information has numbed our mind's ability to feel impressed**. Everyday our brain's surprise threshold is pushed to a **new limit**. To counter this affect, we must cater to the right brain using purpose, mission, and dreams. Help your client understand **your why**, and you will solidify both the left and right brain arguments.

To help ensure your audience will take your content seriously, try to abide by the **Flesch Reading Strategy**: One idea per sentence, single syllable words, short sentences, ask and answer questions, use as many pronouns as you can. While sentences should be short, articles should be **long**. Every major study related to article lengths suggest that **longer is better**.

Your article and email subjects may be the only thing your audience reads. Remember to put your greatest benefit (just **one**) in the subject. The benefit should be housed in a **question**. The question should **challenge your reader's current**

view, but remember to connect with your reader at the beginning of the article with your own skepticism on the topic (to help create **credibility**). If you can hook them within the first paragraph using a dramatic statement or authority, it will be easier to **keep them engaged**.

Email Template:
Subject: *VeloCloud Vs Viptela?*
Email Body: *We asked executives across the industry about why they chose VeloCloud or Viptela for their SD-WAN and here is what they responded with:*

Email Strategy: Every email in a sideways sales letter is crucial. If you break your audience's confidence just **once**, you may lose them **forever**. It's important to add **value** and avoid wasting their time.

14. **Growing Existing Accounts**: One of the fastest sources of growth for your company should always **come from existing accounts**. You will always enjoy a lower growth cost through your existing accounts. To achieve this growth, there are a few important points to consider. The main growth will come from **exceptional service**. To achieve exceptional service with your clients, you must be **proactive**. There will always be times when the client asks for something, but it **should be an exception and not a rule**.

If you can accurately **predict** what your client needs and make ongoing recommendations, your service will be exceptional. **If your service becomes exceptional, you will enjoy higher referral rates and easier up-sells.** How do you become proactive? Watch for **trends**, read industry magazines, keep track of new regulations, and watch for changes at these companies using services like Google Alerts.

In addition to being proactive there are a few details you can employ to create a positive customer experience:

- Don't screen calls
- Answer calls quickly
- Make it easy to reach you
- Answer calls using their **full name**
- Make everyone responsible and accountable for solving problems
- Fix problems and follow-up
- Document problems for future prevention

There may be unpleasant aspects of your interaction with clients (paying the bill, checking in, etc.). Your clients will primarily remember two things from their interaction with you: the **best** and **worst** part. If you get the less joyful parts out of the way **first**, the best part of the experience will be even **better**.

The **Ansoff Matrix** (see below) will help you determine whether new or existing customer acquisitions are appropriate for you.

	Current Offerings	**New Offerings**
New Customers	Offer existing services to new clients	Offer new services to new clients
Existing Customers	Offer existing services to existing clients	Offer new offerings to existing clients

Email Template:
Subject: *Recommendations*
Email Body: *I wanted to run a few ideas by you that I've seen other companies use that works really well. Can we setup a call next week?*

Email Strategy: Most up-sell emails label the discussion as "checking in" or "catching up". More effective emails will discuss recommendations and ideas. Based on experiments and insights you gain from other clients, you should have enough recommendations to help your client on a quarterly basis.

15. **Comics:** Getting your prospects attention can be difficult. To help overcome your prospect's high attention threshold, deliver your message in the form of a **comic**. Rather than copying someone else's creation, it's best if you can **build a new comic from the ground up**. Hire a designer on upwork.com. Another great resource for comic designs is your local college. Reach out to the professors and ask them to share the opportunity with their class.

Your design should implement **subtle reminders of you and your business**. You may consider having your designer use your face or company's logo. Don't worry about your text, this is something you can change down the road. As you share your comic (usually via email) try to add a little customization. Are there any recent events that you can mention, your prospect's company name, their competitors, etc.

Email Template:
Subject: Check this out
Email Body: I thought you might get a kick out of this:

Email Strategy: To avoid scaring away your prospect, the email is simple and friendly. You will likely get an email saying: "Thank you" or "I loved it". Your follow-up email should be simple like:

"I'm glad you liked it". This dialogue will be crucial to continue future conversations that can open doors, ask questions, and run experiments.

16. **Squeeze Pages**: Any campaign is only as effective as the audience's interest to consume your communications. If you send a survey and no one responds, or you share a case study, but the email never gets opened, it will be difficult to continue any campaign. Squeeze page sales strategies enable you to **convert raw email addresses into avid readers.**

A squeeze page is any **online form that asks for your email in exchange for an incentive.** The captured emails are added to your sideways sales letter, enabling you to communicate your company's value effectively again and again.

You may be asking what kind of incentive do I have to offer to get someone to share with me their email address? The first rule of thumb is to offer a **specific** value. For example, I could share a book about how SD-WAN impacts IT Security, but a more attractive incentive would be how SD-WAN impacts IT Security for Credit Unions. The more exclusive your audience is, the higher your response rate will be.

A few squeeze page options are:

- Webinars
- E-Books
- Market Trends
- Newsletters
- White Papers
- Email Courses
- Pricing Sheets
- Case Studies
- Interviews
- Tips
- Live Events
- Book Summaries

Emails **should not be sent more than once a week**. If you don't have something truly valuable to share, **don't send it. A single email can destroy your audience indefinitely**. Additionally, **informal** non-HTML emails are **most effective. Newsletters are counterproductive** because not only do they cause your audience to tune out, but if your audience does take the time to read it, there is **no longer an incentive for them to go to your website**. The short and sweet informal email should give them just enough information that will encourage them to visit your website.

One of the most valuable emails you can offer will consist of a **prospecting list for your audience.** You wouldn't offer this every week, but if you offer a list once a month, you will keep your audience on the edge of their seat. Overall, the email content should feel related to each other, creating a seamless conversation broken up into individual emails. Everything will always be in the form of a trojan horse: your value proposition is always disguised through valuable information.

The primary purpose of this email cadence is **timing**. You never really know when your customer is ready to buy, but if you are **consistently** gaining their mindshare, you will always be in front of the client when the timing is right. Your greatest challenge is to **ensure that they continue to listen to your story**, which depends on your ability to provide value each and every time you connect with them.

Email Template:
Subject: Books
Email Body: I recently compiled a summary of every book in the hotel industry and thought you might find it helpful. Let me know if you would like a copy.

Email Strategy: Here we want to provide the most powerful value we can muster and hope it's strong enough to merit the prospect's email. Like any email campaign, it needs to be simple in order to avoid losing our audience too early.

17. **Competitor Customers**: You may at some point dreamed of uncovering a list of your competitor's **dissatisfied clients** and calling each of them outlining how you can solve the very problem your competitor has created for their business. In this section we are going to **show you where this list of dissatisfied clients exists**.

    Google maps is a treasure trove of information. When you visit your competitor's Google maps page, you will find a list of reviews. The reviews will provide valuable information about what your competitor's clients like and dislike about their service. It's important to learn from both aspects of the reviews, but from a prospecting standpoint, we want to focus on the **bad reviews**. Each review will have either a name and or business associated with the review.

    With the bad review in hand, you can simply look the individual up on LinkedIn and reach out to them. Your initial contact will not be an **offering rather a question about their experience**. Rather than trying to talk them in to trying your service, offer them a free trial and prove to them why your service is better.

Email Template:

Subject: Google

Email Body: I came across your review of #Company# on Google and wanted to thank you. Did you end up switching providers? Do you have any recommendations on companies that work?

Email Strategy: Once you have identified a dissatisfied client, finding out if there still dissatisfied is a great starting point. Like other email strategies, we want to initiate a dialogue and find out what's going on. The public Google review helps form a bridge to warm introduction with a strong context.

18. **Social Selling:** In our chapter on LinkedIn, we have covered most aspects of social selling. There is one particular social strategy outside of LinkedIn that we need to address. Your prospect's attention and time has been democratized across multiple platforms and websites. Rather than competing with these markets, it's more effective to capitalize on their efforts.

Whether on LinkedIn, Twitter, news articles, YouTube and virtually any blog or site you will find a **comment section**. Within Google or any search platform you can identify sites that discuss **topics related to your business**. In the comment section you can comment and include a link back to your site.

How you comment will be important when executing this strategy. It needs to feel **natural and valuable**. It should involve an opinion and content that can add to the article.

This strategy is best executed using an intern. The easiest way to hire an intern is to ask a professor at a college to announce the internship in class or to send an email about the opportunity.

It's worthwhile to invest in website tracking tools to detect who is visiting your site based on their IP address. You should also track your progress using Google Analytics to ensure you're getting a good return on your investment.

Your website will always experience three types of visitors:

- Ready to buy
- Just Browsing
- Unsure

All three website visitors have one thing in common: 70% of the time they **can't find what they're looking for** on your site. Often times our prospects can't find what they're looking for because we are trying to cater to all three groups at the same time. Successful websites focus on visitors who are ready to buy rather than the fence sitters.

Websites should avoid scrolling whenever possible. If you can't avoid scrolling, important information should exist on the page without the user having to scroll down to see it (avoid horizontal scrolls all together). A white background will not only make downloads faster, but enable users to more easily navigate your page.

19. **Job Selling:** Sometimes getting responses to cold emails can be daunting. It's very likely that your email was read (or at least seen) before it was archived by your prospect. In order to get prospects to respond, **you need to start the conversation about something that interests them rather than something about you.**

Among all the experiments I have run for email response rates, job offers **have one of the highest response rates**. You don't need to go and hire your prospects though in order to generate a few sales; rather you need to find someone in your LinkedIn network who is hiring and ask permission to recommend a few candidates.

With this permission, you can now move forward by contacting as many prospects as you want about the job to see if they know anyone that is looking or a good fit. The response **creates a dialog** and an ongoing obligation for your prospects to respond to future emails (**this is your foot in the door**). Once a dialog has been established, you can employ a survey, experiment, and or an opinion-based sales strategy.

Email Template:
Subject: Job Opening
Email Body: *I have a friend that is looking for a new IT Manager. Do you know anyone that you could recommend?*

Email Strategy: This email may feel a little light, but it's the lack of details that will encourage a follow-up from the prospect. They may ask where or what company. Any response will be helpful.

20. **Reverse Marketing Emails:** It's easier to get a response from your prospects **if they email you first**. Getting your prospects to email you may seem hard, but it's easier than you think. Most companies have a newsletter or email updates you sign up for.

    Lots of great information is shared in these communications. You may hear about product launches, new hires, office moves, acquisitions, and more. As you learn about upcoming initiatives for your prospects, **reply to the newsletter, but add your prospect's email** (find it at: upsellreport.com) as a **carbon copy** to the reply.

When you copy more than one individual at a company, you create an internal referral. The **response rates are 3x higher for internal referrals** because if someone ignores your email, the other individual copied on the email will know (hence the carbon copy).

Email Template:
Subject: RE: (Original Subject)
Email Body: I heard about your upcoming product launch. This is really exciting. I've worked with a few other companies in your space that did similar launches and had some issues with their web servers. I can make a few recommendations to make sure you don't have any hiccups. Do you want to jump on a quick call?

Email Strategy: Because we are replying to a bulk email from the company, the sales message can be a little more aggressive here. It's also a good idea to ask questions about what they have done to prepare for the upcoming changes.

21. **Strategic Products:** Sometimes getting in the door is a matter of **leading with the right product**. Rather than trying to overhaul their

entire factory, you may start the conversation about a lightbulb. Likewise, if you're trying to sell a new IT security system, you may start with a simple email filter. The smaller the product you lead with, **the higher the appointment ratio will be.** It's more important to get in the door than it is to sell the right product. You may discover that one of your lead exchange members has the perfect product to lead with. Try to experiment with different product introductions and use the strategy that works best.

Email Template:
Subject: Competitor Phone Numbers
Email Body: I noticed that a few of your competitors are no longer in business. Have you thought about purchasing their phone numbers?

Email Strategy: Acquiring new logos is all about reducing fear. If you are new to them, you need to start with something small. It also needs to be new and attractive enough to make saying yes easy.

22. **Neomania:** In addition to starting with smaller products, talking about **new products** will also lead to more sales appointments. If you can combine a **new small product** (new integration, partnerships, addons, etc.), you will have a much higher appointment ratio. If you track the companies of the vendors your prospects use

(with Google Alerts or Ensable), it will be easy to uncover and discover changes that will be relevant to a Neomania campaign.

Email Template:
<u>Subject</u>: *Did you hear about smart DIDs?*
<u>Email Body</u>: *I've been working with a few of your competitors with smart DIDs and wanted to see if your organization has started using them yet.*

<u>Email Strategy</u>: By nature, individuals want to feel smart (especially in front of others). Often times people will take sales calls just to learn about the latest and greatest technologies.

23. **Executive Assistant Selling:** If you find yourself short on time, hiring an executive assistant is a great solution. In fact, most executive assistants **are free because they pay for themselves**, especially when you get them involved with your sales process.

The best place to find an executive assistant is on Upwork.com. Generally, an executive assistant will run from $5 to $15 an hour. You can start slow by having them work a few hours a week. Not all executive assistants need to speak fluent English. As long as they understand enough to get by, you can **create email templates that will provide proper email responses to your**

campaigns. If an email requires a custom response (outside of your traditional canned responses), have your assistant assign the emails to you for further review.

While executive assistants can help you save time, **their real value comes from response rates**. Most sales experiments have found that executive assistants see **twice the response rate compared to traditional email campaigns**. The reason behind this incredible response rate is that **people take you more seriously when an you have an executive assistant**. Most sales strategies can be adapted to an executive assistant sales strategy.

In addition to helping you get higher response rates, executive assistants can help you clear out your inbox, manage projects, and much more. The book **"The 4 Hour Workweek"** does an excellent job exploring ways an executive assistant can help lighten your load.

Email Template:
Subject: Justin Chugg
Email Body: I am the executive assistant for Justin Chugg. He asked me to reach out to you about a project they're working on. He was wondering if he could talk to you about running an experiment with your company to test a new ROI model with smarter call paths.

Do you have any availability next week?

Email Strategy: This email carries a little more text than most. When using an executive assistant, it's easier to expand the length of the email because you already earned their attention from the first line in the email. The subject line also helps engage the client because they want to know who "Justin Chugg" is and why there is an email about him.

24. **Pricing Sheets:** At some point you have relied on a service like Orbitz to simplify your purchasing journey. **Pricing consolidation** is an extremely valuable content tool that will enable you reach more clients and opportunities.

    Not all pricing sheets create value, but when done correctly, they will be one of your most effective **sales tools**. The key ingredients to any price sheet involve the following:

    - Simplifying data
    - Pricing updates once every two to three months
    - Comparisons should be limited to two categories
    - Use a PDF/Physical Booklets
    - Multiple relevant products
    - Commentary should be included in a coversheet or email body

Here is a sample pricing sheet for bandwidth:

Providing pricing for every relevant product your prospect's purchase, will **compound** the value of your pricing booklet. The burden of creating an extensive booklet should be shared across each member of your lead exchange.

Vendor:	Avg Price Per Mbps	Avg Customer Rating:
Gray Internet	$15.4	4.5
Yellowstone Bandwidth	$35	4.4
Hidden Vendor	$22	4.1
Bandwidth Experts	$22	4.0
Direct Internet	$15	3.8
Communication Inc	$18	3.1
Help Bandwidth	$19	3.9

Email Template:
Subject: *Pricing Updates*
Email Body: *I've been monitoring the pricing for local technology vendors lately and wanted to share a few updates with you (see attached).*

Bandwidth TTY currently has a promo you should look at (it probably won't last long)

Let me know if you have any questions :)

<u>Email Strategy</u>: An effective sales strategy is an **ongoing sales** strategy. Not only do price sheets provide significant value, but their regular updates make it easy to maintain mindshare with your prospects.

25. **Awards:** One of the first items you will see on your client's literature or website are their awards. The placement of these awards reflects their importance and value for your clients. In this strategy we leverage this unprecedented desire your prospects have for awards to create sales opportunities.

To create the strategy, we need to create awards. Here are a few examples of awards you could create for your prospects:

- Product Innovation
- Organization Recovery
- Sales or Revenue Generation
- Most Innovative Company
- Innovation of the Year
- Corporate Social Responsibility Program
- Most Valuable Product
- Most Valuable Service
- Transformation of the Year
- Executive of the Year

- Manager of the Year
- Consultant of the Year
- Outsource Partner of the Year
- Young Entrepreneur of the Year

You will need to create a fair and transparent methodology for distributing the awards. The easiest way is to leverage public data to help you determine the recipients of each award. There are three main sources for award data: Indeed, Glassdoor, and Google Maps. Each of these organizations share public reviews of companies and even provide categorical data to back up the statistics (see examples below).

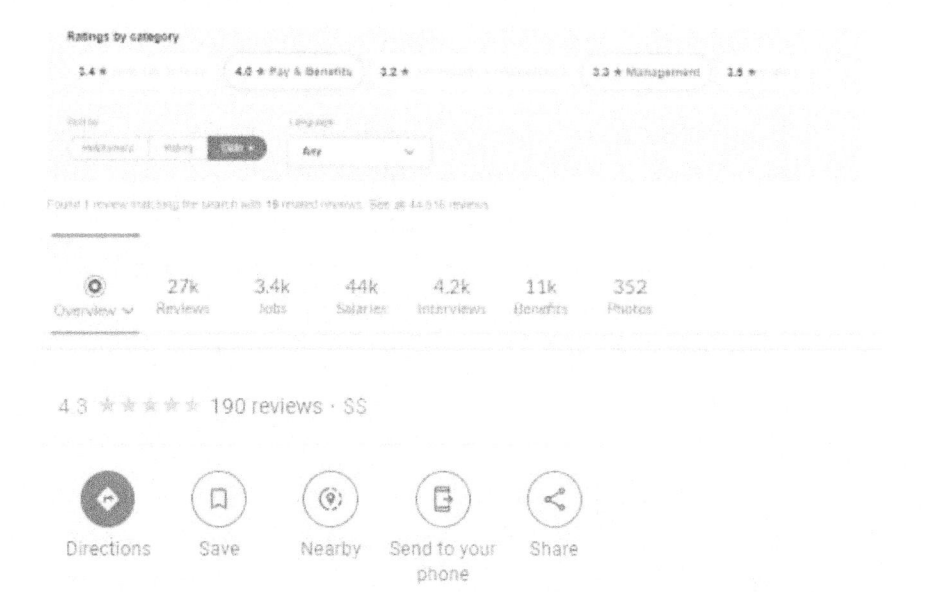

Awards can be divided into four main categories: Geographical, Industry, Company Size, and Founding Date. By creating smaller categories of awards, you will be able to extend more awards to more companies, enabling you to connect with more prospects. In addition, you can create a top five or top ten group called the circle of excellence to help include more companies.

In order to translate awards into sales, you will need to leverage categorical data (the details behind the stats). This will enable you to learn "why" a company was chosen. Based on this data, you will need to determine how your services can enable this "why" for other organizations.

For example, on Glassdoor, many of the employee complaints involves a lack of work life balance. This may require a human resources expert, IT security, and or remote technology, enabling employees to enjoy more freedom and allow the company to achieve a higher level of productivity.

To execute this strategy, you will want to leverage internal referrals. An internal referral is someone other than the decision maker who will become your advocate for your solution. For example, if human resources would like to improve their

Glassdoor rating, they will need technology. They do not purchase the technology to accomplish this goal, but they can become your advocate; therefore, your target for this campaign is the individual that technology helps and not the individual who purchases/implements the service.

This strategy works well with online webinars. You will begin by creating a distro list of companies that would all potentially qualify for the award. A quarterly email highlighting who won should be shared with a follow-up webinar to discuss best practices.

To help legitimize your awards, make sure to include ways for your prospects to highlight their award:

Trophies
Graphics
Video Interviews
Photos
Plaques
Picture Frame Certificates
Inbound Links

Email Template:
Subject: Award Case Study
Email Body: My team has recently reviewed the gaps that exist between the top insurance companies in Alabama

compared to the lowest ranking insurance companies and found one area that stands out: Work Life Balance.

Top performing insurance companies made it possible for employees to maintain a flexible schedule anywhere at any time while at the same time earning higher customer reviews. To achieve this lofty achievement, companies had to invest in better reporting, IT security, and collaboration tools.

Join us next Friday for a full review of how to implement a full-scale life balance solution and to learn more about what companies are doing today to cater to the latest generation of workers.

<u>Email Strategy</u>: Hopefully the award emails have generated enough interest to catch your prospect's attention again with the webinar email. We want to give them enough information to help them make an informed decision about joining the webinar, but not enough to ignore it. When they register for the webinar, make sure you sign them up for an opt-in list to form an ongoing dialogue with them using a sideways sales letter.

26. **Volunteerism**: Sales is not always easy, but volunteerism **makes sales both effective and enjoyable. Volunteerism creates awareness and relationships using community service**. With volunteerism you can be both **proactive and productive**. It is also one of the most

effective **outbound calling strategies for any business**.

While volunteerism is primarily a **service project**, it is also a marketing campaign. Every month you should dedicate **10% of your time (roughly two days/month)**. Your objective is to find companies who may be struggling or need direction in your area of expertise. For example, if you offer technical advice, you could act as their CIO for a day and help provide direction. You could also offer training, audits, disaster recovery plans, or any other service that you believe would be of value.

Rather than ask companies if they need your service, ask for referrals. This is where the marketing aspect of this strategy comes into play. At this point you reach out to your prospects asking them for referrals. The advantage of this angle is that your prospects not only **begin to understand what you do, but they also see your character as someone who wants to help**. It's important to be specific in what you're offering. They may not have someone in mind right away, but that's ok, because you can use that **as an excuse to follow up with them in the future**. In a way this acts as a version of the sideways sales letter.

You may create a refrigerator magnet they can put in their breakroom to help them keep in mind anyone who can use your service. Ultimately this will create a strong **referral network** and a chance to give back to the community. If you have formed a lead exchange, this is the perfect opportunity for you to involve your lead exchange members.

Volunteerism is a great way to help strengthen your company's **character**, give back to the community, and communicate on a regular basis **your value proposition** to your prospects. It is also one of the greatest referral systems ever created. If your team is struggling with the fear of outbound calls, volunteerism will instantly help them overcome this challenge.

To help your volunteerism campaign become more viral, help your audience identify triggers that will lead them to your business. For example, if you work well with hotel clients, let your network know that if they run into anyone that has a hotel to let you know. **The more specific the trigger, the more likely someone will think of you.** Three dimensional objects can help reinforce your triggers. Going along with the hotel example, think of a giveaway that will remind prospects of a hotel: pillows, keychains, pictures, etc.

Many companies use mission statements, but **until you employ volunteerism as a strategy, mission statements will lack**. Volunteerism enables your product to have purpose in the lives of your employees and that **purpose** will change the very nature of their character and the reason why they do what they do.

Email Template:
Subject: *New Project*
Email Body: *Next January we are looking for an opportunity to help the local community here by providing free IT advice to businesses in the area.*

Do you know of any companies that may be struggling? Thanks in advance for your help!

Email Strategy: We want to use an upcoming date or month in these emails to create a sense of urgency. We also leave the content a little ambiguous hoping that the prospect will ask for more information.

There are two main reasons prospects will open your emails:

1. Utility: Clear Subject
2. Curiosity: Vague Subject

Subject Lines should begin with the most important

information and keep the subject line as short as possible.

Appointment setting strategies should leverage the **hill climbing** approach. Rather than constantly switching strategies, continue to **test different versions of the same strategy** while at the same time always exploring a new strategy simultaneously. Your possibility for success can be calculated using the **Laplace's law, which states that your possibility for success (s) in (a) attempts is (s+1)/(a+2).** There is always a chance that a future attempt will not succeed, but your overall success rate will be based on this formula.

You don't need a mathematical formula to know where to get started though. The best approach (known as the **heuristics approach**) is to use **intelligent guess work.** Start with your **gut** and let the **numbers lead the way.**

CHAPTER 6: SALES INTELLIGENCE

It doesn't matter how good your sales strategy is if your timing is off. It's very difficult to sell someone an office building or a new server if they just purchased it. You probably already know a few sales triggers that precede most of your sales, but don't know how to identify them. In this section we will discuss tools and resources you can use **to predict sales with sales intelligence**.

Chances are you are already spreading out your email and phone campaigns (it would be difficult to execute all of them in a single day). Timing helps stack the odds in your favor by prioritizing rather than randomizing. Timing should never replace campaigns, but rather enhance them.

I. **Office Moves:** Before companies vacate their existing office space, many things begin to happen. The first of which is their existing space is put on the market in order to backfill the space quickly. If you can identify who is in the building and who is moving (loopnet.com), it will be easy to predict who your next target is. It is also possible to track the local addresses in your area or those of your customers using Google Alerts: site:loopnet.com/Listing #Address#

Office Moves usually have a wide variety of opportunities for everything from furniture, construction, internet, phone service, and many other opportunities. If you focus on office moves, you will need to form a lead exchange to take advantage of these opportunities.

II. **Profile Changes:** Technically this event falls under our LinkedIn section, but it's important to recognize this timing event as a sales opportunity. When people update their profile, read in between the lines to determine what are they trying to accomplish. 80% of the time profile changes are early signs of a future job changes. When someone updates their profile, this is a good opportunity to ask them if they are open to new job options. They may also feel their job is at risk and a safety net sales strategy would be an attractive solution.

To track profile changes, use LinkedIn and or Google Alerts: site:linkedin.com/in/#Profile#". The #Profile# should be replaced with the actual profile of the individual you want to track. This only works if their profile is public (most are). You are limited to tracking individual profiles (you can use site:linkedin.co/in without the profile component, but Google will limit the amount of data you see.

III. **Construction Projects:** Like Office Moves, construction projects are an excellent opportunity to find new opportunities. Construction projects can be found on Loopnet.com, or using Google Alerts: site:loopnet.com/Listing "New Construction". Your primary focus should be on building relationship with the agent who is trying to fill or sell the building space. As an expert in identifying companies moving out of buildings, this would be the perfect synergy to help add value and create relationships with new real-estate agents.

IV. **Software Changes:** Software plays a pivotal role for any company. Due to the nature of cloud applications, all software solutions do not function independently. Some require secure internet connections, optimized internet connections, phone integrations, etc. As companies implement new software, it's important to explore ways to help them leverage the software to its greatest potential (workforce optimization). To track software changes, you can follow specific companies on Ensable.com/follow

V. **Venture Capital:** Funding goes hand in hand with sales. Before venturing into venture capital opportunities, you should be prepared with ROI models from your experimental sales. Anyone that can show how their product helps company grow faster will be a consistent winner among venture capital organizations. Finding companies receiving venture capital is via news or websites like Crunchbase.

VI. **Vendor Outages:** Services like downdetector.com can identify technology vendors who have let their clients down. In addition, you can see when these vendors have security breaches, mergers, and significant business changes that may impact your clients.

VII. **Disasters:** The number of natural disasters is increasing each year. Some disasters come with a warning (hurricanes) and others without any warning (earthquakes). Services like weather.com can help you create alerts to stay ahead of upcoming challenges and work with companies who may be in the path of disaster. Services like Google Alerts can also supply a stream of companies affected by flooding, earthquakes, fires, and robberies.

Even when companies are not in immediate danger, tools like floodtools.com can help you identify companies that are most at risk for floods.

Most businesses affected by disaster will need to

make significant purchases and changes to adapt and survive. **Preparing products and services to help companies get back up and running quickly will help you win more opportunities here**. It is also helpful to team with commercial insurance brokers, disaster cleanup services, and even local first responders to find ways to help. This also may be a great way to use your volunteerism strategy.

VIII. **Jobs:** Every company has a choice to make when it comes to hiring: to outsource or to hire internally. Companies that post jobs that match the services you offer have not completely committed to an internal employee just yet. Often times the jobs are for contractors or temporary employees. They may also have an immediate need, but are un able to find someone right away and may need your services as a gap filler.

Often times jobs are posted by HR organizations. HR professionals should be at the top of your list for your lead exchange. HR organizations are at the cross roads for businesses looking for people solutions. Rather than collecting a hiring fee, a residual may be more valuable to your HR partners thanks to the consistent revenue flow.

Jobs also shed valuable light into a company's internal needs. There may be a specific phone system, software, or technology listed as a requisite in the job description. Searching for jobs that have hard to find requisites will be easier to sell to. You can track jobs that have specific keywords using the following Google Alert query: site:linkedin.com/jobs/view #Keyword#

IX. **New Executives:** It's been found that **60% of an individual's budget is normally spent within the first six months of employment.** Identifying individuals who have started a new job is a treasure trove of opportunities. Each job change creates a chain reaction of events. Normally the individual who started the new job has left another job that was also recently filled by another person and so on. Referencing the person who just left the job is enough to start a conversation with anyone who has recently filled the position.

The easiest way to initiate these conversations is extending congratulations and **asking them about what their plans are**. The best source for job changes is LinkedIn Sales Navigator or Google Alerts.

X. **Bad News:** The parable of the prodigal son is an excellent illustration of timing. The wise father did not force his immature son to make the right decision. **He waited** until the son learned his lesson and came back to him seeking help and refuge. Businesses act in the same way. You may find it difficult to convince businesses to change and adopt new solutions, but it isn't until things aren't going well that **the timing is right**.

This particular timing element is best used in conjunction with an experimental sales strategy. The easiest way to identify these opportunities is via Google Alerts or Ensable. In Google Alerts, you can add any of the following keywords below and lookup the companies that appear in your news feed each morning.

- Locations Closed
- Bankruptcy
- Restructuring
- Cut Staff
- Cut Workforce
- Layoffs
- Cuts Jobs
- Staff Reduction
- Furlough

CHAPTER 7: MEETINGS

It's a lot of work to secure an appointment. Increasing your ability to win deals depends greatly on your ability to secure appointments, but also **to close the deal**. In this section we will discuss a few techniques that will **increase your ability to close more deals** while in a meeting.

I. **First or Last?** Should you present first or last? Whether you go first or last depends on the timing **between** presentations. If the presentations are back-to-back, you should be the **first** to present. This will help you distort the perception your prospects have of your competitors. If there is more than a week between presentations, its best if you go **last** in order to leave a lasting position and ultimately increase your chances of winning the deal.

II. **How Many Options?** Research suggests that customers who are shown **one** option buy 10% of the time. Customers who see **two** options (including your competitor's product) buy 66% of the time. More than two products will drop the close ratio **significantly**. The research suggests that the client wants to feel secure about their decision by **comparing** it to something else, but if too many options are presented, they feel **overwhelmed**.

In general products and solutions are complex solutions to complex problems. **Our ability to compare complex solutions is limited** and will create a stressful scenario in the brain. To avoid mental **meltdowns**, we need to provide information in the format our brains prefer. We need to begin by **priming the brain and creating a relevant structure to work with**. For example, if you were selling a car, you could show statistics on the average price of cars before you show any options. The two options presented (also known as **dualole persuasion**) need to be in the same realm, but at the same time vastly different. **When two comparative items are too similar, your brain will suffer a brain freeze**. In order to demonstrate the differences between two products, focus on **clearly defined values and benefits**.

III. **Hot or Cold Drink?** Unless it's hot outside, you should always offer a **warm drink (like hot chocolate)**. The warmth of the drink has been proven to place the **nervous system at ease**, helping the decision process to go **smoother**.

IV. **How Should You Sit?** It doesn't matter so much how you sit as long as it **mimics the prospect**.

This has shown to significantly increase close ratios, but always make sure that your way to mimic is subtle.

V. **Morning or Afternoon?** If you can schedule a meeting, is it more likely to be successful in the morning or the afternoon? Due to the fact that your **brain is fresher in the morning, you are more likely to get a yes early on in the day rather than later.** As the day goes on, your ventral lateral prefrontal cortex wears down and **loses its decision-making abilities.** The ventral lateral prefrontal cortex is like a set of breaks that has limited abilities. As the day goes on, its resources become **depleted**. Attempting to make a decision when these resources are depleted strain the resources further causing the prospect to **postpone** the decision. In fact, scientists have found that stressful situations can induce autistic like mindsets. The perceived fear of change will be augmented and more often than not, your clients will choose the status quo.

VI. **Left or Right Side?** Dr Luca Tommasi and Daniele Marzoli from the University Gabrile D'Annunzio ran an experiment asking favors in both the **right** and **left** ears to determine if their success rate would be influenced by the ear they approached. In the end they discovered that the **right ear** was much **more effective** for securing favors from their test subjects.

VII. **Soft or Hard Chairs?** If you have the opportunity to host your prospects, you can help influence the environment that will help them make a decision in your favor. **Soft chairs will help put your prospects at ease** while hard chairs will cause them to feel tense and think twice about their decisions.

VIII. **Smells?** Using nearly identical retail stores, one scented and the other unscented, the scented store had a **significantly higher success rate compared to the unscented store**.

IX. **How to Persuade?** The ability to **change one's perspective is at the heart of the meeting**. If your client was ready to buy, you would be meeting with them to sign the contract, not sell the product. The art of changing someone's opinion is easier than you think. It will require you to **entertain both the left and right hemispheres of the brain**. At the heart of the persuasion process is **novelty**. The mindset will never change without a **fresh new perspective**. If your prospect **does not learn something new from you, there perspective will not change**. Novel insights will lead your customer to **come to their own conclusion**. If you make the conclusion for them, they will not adopt the new perspective. In order to avoid trampling on their conclusion process, **you need to provide information without conclusions**. The most effective strategy for leading your customer to their own conclusions is by avoiding the mistake of offering your opinion. **Let graphs, statistics, evidence, and stories <u>speak for themselves</u>**.

Prospects who come to their own conclusions are <u>more likely</u> to buy from you. **The elaboration likelihood model suggests that there are two paths to persuasion: Logic and association**. Logical persuasion employs **statistics** and **graphs** where association **connects** arguments to existing beliefs using similarities, positive images, cues, etc. While **both strategies should be used**, long-term change and persuasion resistant conclusions **are most likely to be achieved through high-thought logical strategies**. If statistics are packaged using examples (stories), it will evoke emotion, strengthening the argument further.

To further enhance your logical explanation strategy, remember to **expand your list of evidences**. The **length-implies-strength heuristic has shown that additional evidence has a low level of diminishing returns**; the more evidence you can provide, the more persuasion power you will have.

X. **How to Create Desire?** Your customer needs to first understand why they need your product before you can take them on the buying journey. The customer's buying journey can be broken down in to four steps known as the **transtheoretical model**: ignorance, contemplation, planning, and action. Creating desire is the process to move your client from the ignorance stage to the contemplation phase.

To initiate this process, you need to **focus on existing fears** rather than trying to create new ones (the latter is much harder to do). The formula for desire starts with **tension**, which comes when one of our basic needs (survival, free from pain, feeling connected to others, comfort, competition, protect others, and social approval) is not met. Rather than addressing this from a corporate level, it is more effective to uncover the decision maker's **personal tensions**. Are they afraid of losing their job? Are they concerned with how others perceive them in the workplace? Do they need a raise? Do they need to protect their employees?

While the risk associated with the fear may be low, the way we present the risk factor will influence how seriously the prospect considers the risk. If your client has a three percent chance of going bankrupt due to a security breach, it would be more effective to state that three out of a hundred businesses will go bankrupt who experience a security breach. The latter example will feel more real and have a larger impact on their fear.

The purpose of this exercise is not to have your prospect tell you their problems, **but for you to help them see hidden problems**. You need to understand their business and industry well enough to perceive problems that **your prospect is unaware of**, but are **real**. Surveys and experiments will provide you with the insights and answers to help fuel this discussion and ultimately provide **real value**.

The most effective strategy for helping your prospects visualize their problems is through **rhetorical questions**. By nature, our brains our **hard wired to answer questions**. Rhetorical questions are more effective than traditional questions because the prospect can answer their question (this forms an open loop in the reader's mind) in the **quite state of their mind without the influence of others who may hear the question out loud**. The process of change requires your prospect to <u>act</u>. **Without questions, your prospect will never be involved in the process**. If you require your prospect to answer out loud, the answer will be **influenced by those in the room**, inhibiting their ability to truly see the challenge.

XI. **Physical or Digital Content?** While digital information is typically the standard, if you wish to generate an **emotional attachment to your presentation, physical content (printed documents) will be much more effective**.

XII. **Pricing?** A few cents can significantly influence the outcome of your meeting. The **Odd-Even pricing theory states that odd prices like 33, 91, and 73 signal greater value to your clients compared to whole numbers** (like $10.00). On the other hand, products that exhibit greater **quality** will consist of whole numbers (like $10,000).

XIII. **Font?** Your marketing team will almost always generate beautiful easy to read presentations. While common sense would suggest that this will lead to greater sales, but sales studies suggest that the **more effort your prospect employs in understanding your presentation, the greater the retention rate will be**. More laborious fonts will also enhance the product's **perceived value**.

CHAPTER 8: PRACTICAL APPROACH

Congratulations on making it this far in the book. I realize we have covered a lot of ground, so I hope this chapter will bring all of the concepts we have discussed together. Unlike the previous chapters that give you advice and options, this chapter is going to outline what all of these principals look like in an actual sales strategy.

The first step in forming a strategy will involve selecting a target audience. We want our prospects to align vertically and via their **expectations**. In other words, we shouldn't talk to companies within the same vertical that have different service preferences. It's possible to identify companies who meet both of these criteria by looking for common denominators. For instance, you may look at the average household income local to your prospects area. You may also identify vendors they use. Different vendors have different value propositions. If one vendor leans more towards quality while the other vendor prefers value, you can use that as a common identifier within your market to find prospects that align with your values.

In this example, we will be targeting high end dental offices. To begin, I need to form a lead exchange (or networking group). I am going to limit my networking group to five individuals in order to make it easier to manage. The members of my team will consist of the following:

1. Software company that specializes in the dental industry (CRM, Call Center, Accounting, Etc.)
2. Wholesale Dental Supplier
3. Dental Equipment Manufacturer/Vendor
4. Loan Officer
5. Technology Consultant (myself)

Not everyone on our team (like the loan officer) will have an official sales title, but they will be someone that is already proactively looking for new prospects. They will also need to compliment and add value to each member of the team. For instance, when a dentist needs to purchase new equipment, the loan officer can help manage the loan process.

Each member will be expected to contribute $100 a week to participate in the group. The $100 payment will pay for a dedicated sales resource (executive sales assistant) (try upwork.com to find a dedicated resource) that will be primarily responsible for new sales opportunities. Each member will pay $100 for a five-hour prospecting block each day of the work week.

The executive sales assistant will be responsible for the following tasks:

- Building Lead Lists
- LinkedIn Activity
- Emailing Lists
- Answering Emails
- Scheduling Appointments
- Base Management (up-sells)

For this campaign we will use the following sources to build our lead lists:

- **Win Back** Lists (lost clients from the software vendor, manufacturer, and wholesale supplier)
- Clients found on **Google reviews** for the competitors of our group members
- Relevant **LinkedIn connections**

With the list in hand, the executive assistant will now initiate a soft contact campaign via **LinkedIn**, strategically connecting each group member to every potential contact at every prospect. These connections will establish a **soft hook** that we can leverage in the future. The executive assistant will also be responsible for engaging (liking) content produced by these connections and clicking on their LinkedIn profiles on a **regular interval**.

Messaging Templates will need to be created by the team to help the executive assistant have the optimal message for potential prospects. For instance, each member would create a message to send when creating a LinkedIn connection, regular LinkedIn messages, profile view follow-ups, etc.

The executive assistant will prioritize their time with the following activities:

1. Inbound Emails
2. LinkedIn Profile View Follow-Ups
3. Anonymous Website Visitors
4. LinkedIn Connecting
5. LinkedIn Engagement
6. Outbound Emails
7. List Building

Some activities will need to be pursued directly by the group that require your expertise. This would include answering difficult email questions from prospects, reviewing prospect's newsletters for opportunities to engage about new opportunities.

The lead exchange members should form a group purchasing solution that provides discounts (in and outside of the lead exchange) to prospects. The purchasing group can start small and expand over time.

The executive assistant will then begin proactively engaging (not selling) to prospects. The initial conversation will ask the prospect about who they recommend for a particular service/vendor a member of the lead exchange represents. Each week the executive assistant will focus on a different product. They will avoid contacting the same prospect within a six-week period (unless a follow-up is involved). Messages can begin on LinkedIn or reference their relationship in an email. We're going to assume that for this industry, most dentists will not respond to LinkedIn emails as much as they would their work email.

The information gathered about vendor preferences and experiences will help form follow-up conversations. For instance, if your prospects use a vendor/competitor from your purchasing group, follow-up with a did you know we can get you a better price for the same service?

As you get to know your prospects, explore potential experiments you can run together. The experiments are most effective with **inexpensive** solutions that are **new**. For example, you may email your prospects and ask them if they would be willing to test a textable phone service for their business. Ask them if you can measure the impact a textable phone number and service would have on **appointments**. You could also measure the impact it has on **sales** as you free up staff members time to up-sell clients and more lucrative dental procedures. You could also test net new appointments by freeing up staff member's time to reach out to past clients about new appointments.

Your executive assistant will use an email that you create for your lead exchange group or for each individual's company. They will present themselves as your executive assistant and will look for opportunities for each team member. Once an appointment is booked, it will be the responsibility of the team to move forward with the opportunity. Each member will try to find ways to involve/recommend other group members to the prospects.

Each experiment will need a case study, which should be shared with industry magazines and directly with all prospects. Each of these emails will form a cadence, highlighting preferred vendors, where to get the best discounts, competitor's experiences with industry products and vendors. As time goes on, you will begin to form a rich archive of lessons that when combined, create a valuable outline for success that your prospects can use. To help augment your credibility and continue developing relationships, these studies should be published as a formal book. Each member of the lead exchange can help write different sections and interview prospects about their expert opinion on the book's topics in order to provide additional depth.

Every positive experiment should be used to engage with every other potential client. Even after you have discovered a successful formula, you will still approach it as an experiment. Case studies and evidence of success will be added to the experiment's proposal to help encourage future adoption. The vendors who you have a positive experience with via the experiments should help **invest** in marketing initiatives using marketing development funds to share the success story with other companies (it will be hard for them to resist not to). We will encourage vendors and industry news sources to share the case study.

Once you dominate the local dental market, expand to other regions, states, and eventually the entire country. If you have truly penetrated/won a majority of these prospects, you can consider moving on to a similar industry like vision, chiropractors, etc.

CHAPTER 9: CONCLUSION

Years ago, a man was awoken by a knock at his door at 3:00 AM. A neighbor whom he did not know had taken the time to warn him about a forest fire that had taken over their neighborhood. After returning to his home later that week he began to fully appreciate the sacrifice his neighbor had made. His home was completely gone along with every other home in the neighborhood. Without this early warning, he and his family would have never made it out alive. As sales professionals our products and services should provide **real value**.

It's very likely that the product in and of itself **does not have much value to your clients**. As a sales professional it's our responsibility to help our clients find and discover the value of our product. **The intrinsic value of our products is <u>us</u>**. We need to fully understand how our product is not only free, but pays for itself by **experimenting** and solving **real problems**. Your customer will buy from you when the value of the product outweighs the cost of the product. The only way they will understand the value of this product is through **you**. Only as you experiment will you begin to develop the true **value** of the product that will outweigh its cost.

The value of any product is how we use it. When complex business products are introduced to companies, it will require **an expert outside of their organization to help them leverage the product for their benefit**. The ultimate sales tool is the **knowledge of how to help others make money** using your products. If you haven't discovered a specific formula or strategy directly related to your product that will not only pay for the product, but help your client save/make money, **you will have a hard time selling**. In the end the argument is about **price vs cost**. The latter reflects the true value of the service/product.

When the stranger knocked on the man's door to warn him of the fire, it was her **insight** of the fire that provided the **value**, that **welcomed** her message. Likewise, **if we do not possess equal insight as the woman, our messages will always become a nuisance rather than a blessing**. It will suck the marrow out of our confidence and drain the energy of our sales team as they attempt to sell something, they cannot articulately describe the value of.

Creating real value almost always requires **making sacrifices**. You will have to decide between features that will benefit one group of customers over the others. You will need to sacrifice understanding one industry over another in order to truly understand your value proposition. In the end the fastest value building tool is built **vertically** not horizontally.

Made in the USA
Columbia, SC
16 September 2024